STARS & STRIPES FOREVER

ALSO BY RICHARD H. SCHNEIDER

Taps: Notes from a Nation's Heart

Freedom's Holy Light: The Statue of Liberty

Why Christmas Trees Aren't Perfect

Christopher Schneider, Cub Scout, at a Memorial Day ceremony in Highland Park, Illinois, circa 1967.

STARS & STRIPES FOREVER

THE HISTORY, STORIES, AND MEMORIES OF OUR AMERICAN FLAG

Richard H. Schneider

Wm

William Morrow

An Imprint of HarperCollins*Publishers*

Grateful acknowledgment is made to reprint the following:

"This Is a Precious Thing" by Deborah Smoot. Copyright © 1991 by Guideposts. Reprinted with permission from *Guideposts* magazine. All rights reserved.
"Something to Remember" by Eleanor V. Sass. Copyright © 1978 by Guideposts. Reprinted with permission from *Guideposts* magazine. All rights reserved.
"My Name Is Old Glory" by Howard Schnauber. Copyright © 1994 by Howard Schnauber. Interview with Howard Schnauber conducted by Rheba Massey. Reprinted courtesy of the Fort Collins Public Library Local History Archive, Oral History Interview of Mr. Howard Schnauber.
Christopher Radko, "Flag." Copyright © 2002 by Starad, Inc., by Christopher Radko.
David Fruge, "The Flag That's Never Flown." Copyright © 1996 by David Fruge.
Master Sergeant Percy Webb, USMC, "I Am Old Glory." Copyright © 1985 by Percy Webb.

For Illustration credits, see page 193.

HarperCollins books may be purchased for educational, business, or sales promotional use. For information please write: Special Markets Department, HarperCollins Publishers Inc., 10 East 53rd Street, New York, NY 10022.

FIRST EDITION

Designed by Nicola Ferguson

Printed on acid-free paper

Library of Congress Cataloging-in-Publication Data
Schneider, Richard H., 1922–
Stars & stripes forever : the history, stories, and memories of
our american flag / Richard H. Schneider.
p. cm.
ISBN 0-06-052537-1
1. Flags—United States—History.
I. Title: Stars & stripes forever. II. Title.
CR113 .S36   2003
929.9'2—dc21   2002043213

03 04 05 06 07 ❖/QW 10 9 8 7 6 5 4 3 2 1

*To all the men and women
who gave their lives for our country
and the flag for which it stands*

Contents

Vexillology: The study of flags and ensigns. A vexillum (plural: vexilla) is a military standard or flag used by ancient Roman troops.

STARS & STRIPES
FOREVER

The Raising of the Colors

*I*n World War II, I served in a Signal Operations Battalion stationed in Normandy, France, during the autumn of 1944. We had been expecting the arrival of radio equipment but it had been delayed by several weeks, so we were forced to stay in a makeshift encampment while we waited. Throughout this enforced idleness there were torrential rains almost every day, with a cold wind to make things even more miserable. And to top it off, we were forced to sleep on the muddy ground, covered only by our blankets and flimsy shelter halves.

Then, right when the cold wet weather and the boredom were getting almost unbearable, our sergeant asked me to accompany him on a trip to our divisional headquarters. I jumped at the chance. We clambered into the open-sided Jeep and took off. For hours we slipped and yawed up a rocky road through a canyon of tall, dark pines. Mud from the ruts was thrown up into our faces, only to be washed away by the steady downpour of rain. Gradually, however, the showers

U.S. Army Corporal Richard Schneider, Belgium, 1944.

tapered off, the road began to level out, and the tall trees gave way to small scrub—we were nearing the headquarters encampment.

And then, as the first faint gleams of sun began to break through the clouds, my heart leaped at a breathtaking sight. There, flying proudly from an almost impossibly tall staff, was an enormous American flag. It was the first time I had seen our flag flying since we had left New York harbor months before. In a flash, the misery of the last few muddy weeks was replaced by one overwhelming thought—Home!

In my mind's eye, I saw my father putting out the flag at

our house every single morning. I saw myself standing in my grade-school classroom, hand over heart while saying the Pledge of Allegiance. I saw my whole family standing on the main street of Oak Park, Illinois, as the Memorial Day parade with its ocean of flags made its way past us . . . and my mother hastily grabbing my cap off my head.

In the billowing fabric of those Stars and Stripes I saw everyone from my life who had nurtured me in some way— relatives, neighbors, teachers, friends—all those people in whom I had placed my trust over the years. Now, in return, they were placing their trust in me and my fellow soldiers as we fought for freedom on foreign soil.

As we all travel these perilous roads today of uncertainty, controversy, and anxiety, I pray that our hearts will still leap every time we look up through the mist to see that our flag is still there.

CHAPTER ONE

Our Flag's Beginnings

*M*oviegoers were moved and inspired as they watched Mel Gibson on horseback gallop across the screen in *The Patriot,* a movie set during the American Revolution. But it wasn't Gibson's horsemanship that thrilled us; it was the American "Betsy Ross" battle flag with its circle of thirteen stars and thirteen red and white stripes he so proudly carried.

Not until I began researching our country's Stars and Stripes did I learn that historians cannot agree if this flag was ever even used by American troops. One can't blame Hollywood for bending history to create an exciting visual moment. They felt that the Betsy Ross flag was something American filmgoers would relate to.

And no wonder. Since 1875 almost every American has become familiar with the well-known painting entitled *The Spirit of '76* portraying a valiant marching threesome: a drummer boy, a bandaged fife player, and an old man proudly marching beside a Betsy Ross flag. Many American historians, however, doubt that Betsy Ross had anything to do with the origins of our flag—but we'll delve into that hornet's nest later.

As much as we revere our national banner, few people are truly familiar with its amazing and colorful history. Some might be familiar with the old "Don't Tread on Me" flag—especially in light of the fact that our American troopships in the Middle East are even now flying that banner. But there's an incredible and fascinating story behind Old Glory that isn't taught in schools—amazing bits of lore, legend, and even falsehoods that surround this symbol of our country.

FLAGS IN ANCIENT TIMES

Flags and banners have been used as symbols for sovereign nations and other organizations since our civilization first began to record its history. As early as 4000 B.C. Egyptian ships sailed under flags indicating their home port. And even the Good Book makes mention of banners: God tells Moses and Aaron that "Every man of the children of Israel shall pitch by his own standard, with the ensign of their father's house. . . ." (Numbers 2:3).

As time passed, flags were flown by a wide range of people and groups, including kings, armies, and cities. Some prominent merchants in the Middle Ages had their own flags designed so that their ships and barges could be identified as they came into the harbor. But it wasn't until the dawn of the sixteenth century that flags were used as symbols of nations or countries. Around 1500, European merchant ships had started to roam farther from their own coastlines in an effort to establish trade with far-flung nations. Flags and banners were flown from their masts to identify them and ensure that they weren't mistaken for ships carrying invading troops.

At this point these vessels were flying the royal colors of the particular king or royal family that they served. However, given the huge number of royals in those days, there were just as many different flags, each one with its own assortment of lions, harps, lilies, or stars and just as many colors. It soon became almost impossible for the lookouts in a port to identify which flag was for which royalty—they would have had to have the equivalent of today's phone book directory to keep things straight.

To solve this confusion, ships began to fly flags that identified their country of origin. (See color insert.) This allowed for a much simpler range of colors and marks, such as the blue and white of France, the red and white of England, and the green and white of Portugal. Though many of these flags have since been embellished, some nations still have simple multicolored flags, such as Germany, the Netherlands, and Spain.

THE FIRST FLAGS IN NORTH AMERICA

Most people today would assume that the first flag to touch the shores of North America was carried by the crew of Christopher Columbus's trio of ships back in the early 1490s. Actually, however, the very first recorded instance of a flag touching the shores of our continent dates from almost five hundred years before, when the keel of a Viking longboat ground onto the large rough stones of a beach in Newfoundland back around A.D. 1000. The ancient Norse explorers of that time flew the Viking banner—a black raven on a white background.

The ships and flags of many other countries were to land on the shores of America in the centuries to come. By far the most significant of these arrivals, however, and the one to carry the most consequences for our country, both good and bad, occurred in 1607.

On May 14 of that year, a small ship, its crew still recovering from the rigors of a trans-Atlantic voyage, slowly tacked into a shallow harbor of Jamestown Island off the coast of Virginia. This vessel, carrying a complement of explorers, entrepreneurs, and artisans, flew the colors of the British Union Jack. It was this flag that flew above the settlements at Jamestown and the later settlements in Plymouth, Massachusetts, and the others that began to dot the coast of the New World. It was the Union Jack that the new Americans proudly raised on the masts of their ships and the flagpoles in the town squares—and it was the Union Jack that only a hundred and fifty years later would become a symbol of oppression and unjust rule from afar.

The British Union Jack had been in existence just a scant four years before it flew over Jamestown, Virginia. Designed in 1603 to represent the nation of the newly unified England and Scotland, the new flag incorporated elements from the banners of the two countries: the red British Cross of St. George (the dragon slayer) and the white Scottish cross of St. Andrew (the venerated brother of the apostle Peter, who was said to have been crucified on an angled cross). (See color insert.)

For many decades the bright colors of the Union Jack brought comfort to the people who settled the wild country of the New World and who later began to establish the centers of commerce and society throughout the eastern third of America. As early as 1750, however, rumblings of complaint began to be heard about the heavy hand of Mother England. Merchants complained of the increasing taxes and levies they were forced to pay. Laws and regulations began to multiply and become stricter as the British attempted to head off any efforts on the part of the colonies to establish autonomy. Ironically, had the British allowed the colonists some local governance and a representative voice in the establishment of new taxes and regulations, they might have avoided any active rebellion and the Union Jack might still be flying throughout our country today. Reasonable heads did not prevail, how-

George Washington Crossing the Delaware, *painted by Emanuel Gottlieb Leutze.*

ever, and the iron bands of British rule clamped even harder. The intimidating presence of red-coated British soldiers grew more prevalent throughout the colonies and any signs of incipient revolt were ruthlessly quashed.

The simmering tension finally came to a head on April 19, 1775, when for the first time colonists raised their own state and militia colors and assembled against the British soldiers on Lexington Green in Massachusetts. One unknown red-coat, probably scared out of his wits by the relentless faces of the oncoming ragtag group of men who showed no fear, fired the first shot—"the shot heard round the world." As of that very moment the Union Jack ceased to represent the people of America.

THE FIRST AMERICAN FLAGS

Historians are unsure which flag the colonists first used to demonstrate their dissatisfaction with British rule. One of the earliest flags flown was inspired by a design by Benjamin Franklin. He had sketched out a rattlesnake that had been cut

An Early Old Glory Flies Again

In the wake of the September 11, 2001, attacks on the World Trade Center and the Pentagon, the U.S. Navy has ordered its fleet to fly the defiant "Don't Tread on Me" flag aboard all its vessels.

The flag, which was modified from a design by Benjamin Franklin and features a rattlesnake against a background of red and white stripes, was never an official flag of the United States. The flag had been used in the days prior to the Revolutionary War as a threatening gesture to the British.

"We are reviving a patriotic symbol from our nation's past to emphasize America's determination in the war on terror," said Navy Secretary Gordon England in a press release following the attack. "The resurrected flag represents an historic reminder of the nation's and Navy's origin and will to persevere and triumph."

into nine pieces, representing the nine colonies. The legend on the drawing read: "Unite or Die." When the revolutionary soldiers were casting about for a design for banners, they recalled Franklin's rattlesnake and used it—only this time the snake was not divided into pieces; it was most certainly a whole snake with its fangs bared, and it carried the more defiant motto, "Don't Tread on Me."

When the Stamp Act was imposed on the colonies in 1765, a group of protesters began to meet under a particular elm tree in Boston to share their views. As their group grew in size and their rebellious nature began to crystallize, they started to refer to themselves as "The Sons of Liberty" and the elm tree beneath which they met became known as the Liberty Tree. Once word of this group reached the British, soldiers rushed to chop the tree down. The Sons of Liberty promptly cut the branches off the hewn tree and set it back up, now calling it the Liberty Pole. It was from this makeshift pole that the first flag to feature red and white stripes was flown. It was a simple affair—a rectangle featuring nine red and white vertical stripes. The stripes represented the nine colonies, just like the nine segments of Franklin's rattlesnake emblem. This flag became known as the Flag of the Sons of Liberty.

Two months after the Battle of Lexington, the rebels laid siege to the "lobsterbacks" in Boston in what became known as the Battle of Bunker Hill. As the local citizenry cheered them on, the small band of revolutionaries took over the battlements on Breed's Hill. Three furious and bloody charges by the redcoats failed to dislodge them—only when their gunpowder ran out did they withdraw. Each show of force by the emboldened rebels provided a shot in the arm to the colonists' morale

DON'T TREAD ON ME

The Gadsden flag.

as they realized they didn't have to stand for unjust treatment.

The flag carried by the colonists that day was known as the New England flag. (See color insert.) It was a red flag with a white canton bearing the image of a pine tree. (A - "canton" is a rectangular portion of a flag, placed in the upper quadrant closest to the staff—e.g., the field of blue with white stars in the American flag is a canton.) Within a few months' time, the New England flag began to sprout up throughout the colonies. Colonial ships flew a variant of this flag—a white flag with a red canton featuring a pine tree. These variants also carried the motto "An Appeal to Heaven" written across the bottom.

Throughout the second half of 1775, Commander George Washington ranged up and down through the colonies, meeting with the leaders of hundreds of local militias and other armed groups. His goal was simple—to organize these ragtag soldiers into one united armed force. After months of

David Martucci

David Martucci is president of the North American
Vexillological Association.

Americans love their flag. It is perhaps the ultimate expression of what it means to be an American. Regardless of political philosophy or opinion, the flag represents us all, and at the same time transcends any attempt to define its symbolism.

The "Stars and Stripes" was born on June 14, 1777, with a single, tersely worded sentence, "Resolved that the Flag of the United States be 13 stripes, alternate red and white; that the Union be 13 stars, white in a blue field, representing a new Constellation."

The entire meaning of the red, white, and blue was left freely to the imagination of the American people, with no specification given to the exact pattern or dimension until President Taft standardized the design in 1912. Nor has there ever been any government-ordained symbolism to believe in.

exhausting work and travel, his efforts finally bore fruit—on New Year's Day of 1776, the Continental Army was formally established, with General George Washington in charge.

One of the first orders of business was to establish the colors under which this new army would fight. Oddly enough, the leaders wanted to include the Union Jack within the new flag as a sign that they were still loyal to England. In spite of

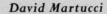

Americans took the flag to heart immediately. We constantly renew its meaning and importance in our lives. It is the most changed flag in the world, having been officially amended twenty-seven times. It is not a static thing. It is dynamic and alive.

Ours was the first to be termed a "national" flag. Before it, only kings and governments and armies had flags. But "Old Glory" belongs to a people, not to a government. Even today, the British Union Jack technically belongs to the crown.

In addition to its obvious symbolism, that of thirteen states grown to fifty, yet one nation, Americans understand the flag in many different ways. Still, we believe in one flag, and how it defines us all. "E pluribus unum." "Out of many, one."

For Americans, the flag is much more than a piece of cloth. We keep it in our hearts. It is the story of who we are, what we believe in, and where we are going—a story that has not yet been fully written.

the bloodshed and destruction that marked these first years of rebellion, the colonists were not yet at the point that they wanted complete freedom from England. They were simply angry at the unfair treatment they had received from the mother country and were demanding a fairer and more autonomous rule.

The new flag was a modification of the British Red Ensign, a maritime flag that featured a red field with the Union Jack in the canton. The red field was changed to a field of thirteen red and white stripes, representing the colonies—now grown in number from nine to thirteen—united in their grievance.

The First Naval Ensign flag—a variant of the New England flag.

This first symbol of the thirteen united colonies was called the Grand Union flag.

The headquarters of the Continental Army was in the town of Somerville, on Prospect Hill just outside of Boston. As the new flag was being sewn, General Washington ordered that a seventy-six-foot-tall flagpole be erected in the yard. Finally, it was all ready. One can picture Washington standing there among his troops in the chill winter wind, watching with a fierce pride—and perhaps a bit of fear at the trials he knew were to come—as the new Grand Union flag was run to the top of the towering pole. This banner of defiance could be seen for miles around, even in Boston, where the British soldiers still held sway.

Unknown to Washington and his men, a missive from King George III to the colonies had just been received in Boston. The message was a rather feeble and much belated attempt on the part of the king to curry favor with the colonists and try to assuage their hurt feelings. Therefore, when the British officers in Boston were informed that the

new colonial army had just raised a huge flag at its headquarters—a flag with the Union Jack featured prominently in
the canton, no less—they assumed that it was a sign that the
rebels had received the king's message and were thus indicating their surrender and subjugation to the crown. The British
forces relaxed and began to congratulate themselves on their
success in quashing the rebellion. Their feelings of confi-
dence and self-satisfaction quickly turned to terror, however,
as only days later they saw the "sign of subjugation" flying
in the front lines of the most determined and ferocious forces
the British army had ever faced.

On July 4, 1776, any lingering sense of loyalty to the
crown was put to rest when the Second Continental Congress
formally adopted the Declaration of Independence, after
weeks of debate and meetings in the sweltering Philadelphia
summer.

It was not until almost a year later, however, that the subject of a national flag arose. Oddly enough, from the time independence was declared to June of the following year—a
period that saw some of the fiercest fighting of the war—the
British Union Jack remained as a prominent element of the
American flag.

June 14, 1777, does not at first seem to have been a particularly significant day in Congress. In fact, if you read the
Journal of the Continental Congress for that date, it appears as
if the senators were simply tending to the mundane business

The Days to Display Your Flag

The flag should be displayed, from sunrise to sunset, on all days when the weather permits. However, the following days are specifically designated as days to fly the Stars and Stripes:

New Year's Day

Inauguration Day

Martin Luther King Jr.'s Birthday

Lincoln's Birthday

Washington's Birthday

Easter Sunday

Patriots Day (April 19)

National Day of Prayer
 (first Thursday in May)

Mother's Day

Armed Forces Day

Memorial Day *(half-staff until noon)*

Flag Day

Independence Day (July 4)

Labor Day

Constitution Day

Columbus Day (October 12)

Navy Day

Election Day

Veterans Day

Thanksgiving Day

Christmas Day

. . . and any other such days as may be proclaimed by the President of the United States.

And don't forget to fly the flag on your state's birthday! (The day it was admitted to the Union is generally considered the holiday in question.)

of government. The real action was taking place only twenty miles away—General Washington had just learned that a massive British flotilla was making its way down the Atlantic coast, intending to land in Wilmington, Delaware.

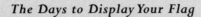

Washington had only a few weeks to mobilize his far-flung troops and get them to Delaware to greet the British.

But back in Philadelphia the wheels of government ground on, in spite of the unseasonable heat that assailed the city. The sun beat down mercilessly on the

The British Red Ensign Flag.

shingled roofs of the statehouse and reflected up from the cobbled streets. The senators within the statehouse tugged at their tight collars and mopped sweat from their brows with the large handkerchiefs that were the fashion, all the while fanning themselves with the countless sheaves of paper that even then seemed to be the hallmark of government.

According to the *Journal* of the Continental Congress, the business conducted that day seemed to be primarily concerned with the Marine Committee. One issue involved directing the Continental Navy to proceed down the Delaware River toward Wilmington to support Washington's efforts there. There was no urgency to this order, however, given that the ships had already taken off two days earlier—it was simply laying a trail of paperwork. Another issue concerned questions raised about the character of the commander of the navy ship *Ranger*. After some debate, it

Alabama (22nd state) December 14, 1819 (5th U.S. flag design/23 stars)

Alaska (49th state) January 3, 1959 (26th U.S. flag design/49 stars)

Arizona (48th state) February 14, 1912 (25th U.S. flag design/48 stars)

Arkansas (25th state) June 15, 1836 (7th U.S. flag design/25 stars)

California (31st state) September 9, 1850 (13th U.S. flag design/31 stars)

Colorado (38th state) August 1, 1876 (20th U.S. flag design/38 stars)

Connecticut (5th of original 13) January 9, 1788** (1st U.S. flag design/13 stars)

Delaware (1st of original 13) December 7, 1787** (1st U.S. flag design/13 stars)

Florida (27th state) March 3, 1845 (9th U.S. flag design/27 stars)

Georgia (4th of original 13) January 2, 1788** (1st U.S. flag design/13 stars)

Hawaii (50th state) August 21, 1959 (27th U.S. flag design/50 stars)

Idaho (43rd state) July 3, 1890 (21st U.S. flag design/43 stars)

Illinois (21st state) December 3, 1818 (4th U.S. flag design/21 stars)

Indiana (19th state) December 11, 1816 (3rd U.S. flag design/20 stars)

Iowa (29th state) December 26, 1846 (11th U.S. flag design/29 stars)

Kansas (34th state) January 23, 1861 (16th U.S. flag design/ 34 stars)

Kentucky (15th state) June 1, 1792 (2nd U.S. flag design/15 stars)

Louisiana (18th state) April 30, 1812 (3rd U.S. flag design/ 20 stars)

Maine (23rd state) March 15, 1820 (5th U.S. flag design/23 stars)

Maryland (7th of original 13) April 28, 1788** (1st U.S. flag design/13 stars)

Massachusetts (6th of original 13) February 6, 1788** (1st U.S. flag design/13 stars)

Michigan (26th state) January 26, 1837 (8th U.S. flag design/ 26 stars)

Minnesota (32nd state) May 11, 1858 (14th U.S. flag design/ 32 stars)

Mississippi (20th state) December 10, 1817 (3rd U.S. flag design/20 stars)

Missouri (24th state) August 10, 1821 (6th U.S. flag design/ 24 stars)

Montana (41st state) November 3, 1889 (21st U.S. flag design/ 43 stars)

Nebraska (37th state) March 1, 1867 (19th U.S. flag design/ 37 stars)

Nevada (36th state) October 31, 1864 (18th U.S. flag design/ 36 stars)

New Hampshire (9th of original 13) June 21, 1788** (1st U.S. flag design/13 stars)

New Jersey (3rd of original 13) December 18, 1787** (1st U.S. flag design/13 stars)

New Mexico (47th state) January 6th, 1912 (25th U.S. flag design/48 stars)

New York (11th of original 13) July 25, 1788** (1st U.S. flag design/13 stars)

North Carolina (12th of original 13) November 21, 1789** (1st U.S. flag design/13 stars)

North Dakota (39th state) November 2, 1889 (21st U.S. flag design/43 stars)

Ohio (17th state) March 1, 1803 (3rd U.S. flag design/20 stars)

Oklahoma (46th state) November 16, 1907 (24th U.S. flag design/46 stars)

Oregon (33rd state) February 14, 1859 (15th U.S. flag design/33 stars)

Pennsylvania (2nd of original 13) December 12, 1787** (1st U.S. flag design/13 stars)

Rhode Island (13th of original 13) May, 29, 1790** (1st U.S. flag design/13 stars)

South Carolina (8th of original 13) May 23, 1788** (1st U.S. flag design/13 stars)

South Dakota (40th state) November 2, 1889 (21st U.S. flag design/43 stars)

was decided to replace the commander with a relatively unknown officer named John Paul Jones.

However, shoehorned in the *Journal* between these two innocuous issues is a short thirty-two-word passage with no explanation or comment. It reads: "Resolved, that the flag of

Tennessee (16th state) June 1, 1796 (3rd U.S. flag design/ 20 stars)

Texas (28th state) December 29, 1845 (10th U.S. flag design/ 28 stars)

Utah (45th state) January 4, 1896 (23rd U.S. flag design/45 stars)

Vermont (14th state) March 4, 1791 (2nd U.S. flag design/ 15 stars)

Virginia (10th of original 13) June 25, 1788** (1st U.S. flag design/13 stars)

Washington (42nd state) November 11, 1889 (21st U.S. flag design/43 stars)

West Virginia (35th state) June 20, 1863 (17th U.S. flag design/35 stars)

Wisconsin (30th state) May 29, 1848 (12th U.S. flag design/ 30 stars)

Wyoming (44th state) July 10, 1890 (22nd U.S. flag design/ 44 stars)

**Denotes the date each of the first thirteen colonies ratified the Constitution of the United States.*

the United States be made of thirteen stripes, alternate red and white; that the Union be thirteen stars, white in a blue field, representing a new constellation."

As simple and as elegant as that. At the time the senators probably viewed the resolution as one among many—simply

The Bennington flag.

one more vote to get through before the hot and grueling day was over. In retrospect, however, these thirty-two words gave birth to the tapestry that represents our country to the world—and we now celebrate every June 14 as Flag Day. Call it Old Glory, the Star-Spangled Banner, the Stars and Stripes, or any of its other nicknames—it still stands for only one thing: the United States of America.

When and where the first Stars and Stripes flew during the Revolution is difficult to pin down. One tradition holds that it was the flag used by the Bennington militia at the Battle of Bennington in southern Vermont on August 16, 1777. Its thirteen stars arch over the number "76." It is considered by some to be the oldest American flag in existence. (You can see it displayed at the Bennington Battle Monument and Historical Association.)

Then there was the flag flown at the battle at Fort Anne, New York. In his journal entry for July 10, 1777, a British officer told how they had defeated the colonists and taken their colors. His description of their flag is very similar to the words used in the June 14 resolution.

Even though it was less than a year old, the government's wheels had already started moving slowly. It wasn't until six years later, in 1783, that the Continental Army was finally supplied with its first shipment of the nation's new flag. By then, of course, the war was over.

The brief June 14 resolution, as elegant as it is, was only the beginning of a long journey in the evolution of our nation's flag. For example, even though the red and white stripes and white stars on a field of blue are specified, there's no mention of proportions, where the stars should be placed, or even whether the stripes should be vertical or horizontal. The story of the American flag is a fascinating tapestry in itself of amazing lore, legends, and little known but true facts.

CHAPTER TWO

Betsy Ross: Did She or Didn't She?

*I*t makes for a charming story, one that many of us read in grade school. Back in May of 1776, on a swelteringly hot day in Philadelphia, three distinguished men walked purposefully along the cobblestones toward a small house on Arch Street. Just a few days before, these men had been appointed to a special task by the fledgling U.S. Congress, and they were now carrying out their commission.

The first of these men was Robert Morris, a wealthy businessman who was helping to finance the American Revolution. The second was General George Washington, the man responsible for winning the war that Morris was funding. The third man was Colonel George Ross, a relative of the person who lived in that small building on Arch Street.

When they arrived at the house, they noted that it also served as an upholstery shop for the woman who owned it— a twenty-four-year-old seamstress named Betsy Ross. Betsy

Could It Be the Original Star?

A small scrap of paper lies in a display case kept in the parlor of the Free Quaker Meeting House on Arch Street in Philadelphia. This bit of paper offers additional conclusive proof—at least to her supporters—that Betsy Ross met with representatives of Congress for the purposes of creating the flag.

The paper is a small five-pointed star. According to the story, Samuel Wetherill, a Quaker like Betsy herself, stopped in to her shop shortly after George Washington and his two companions left. When he saw the star that Ross had snipped out for her visitors, he asked if he might keep it.

Almost a century and a half later, in 1925, the Wetherill family safe was opened after decades of nonuse. When the family went through the various papers contained therein, they came across the star accompanied by a note from Samuel detailing where he had obtained it.

If you don't believe that, you can cut out a five-pointed star with just one snip of a scissors, try it for yourself. Here are the directions:

Take a thin piece of paper 8-1/2" x 10" (or an exact proportion thereof), fold it as indicated and cut yourself a perfect 5-pointed star.

(1) FOLD (2)

8-1/2"

Step 1. Fold an 8-1/2" x 10" piece of paper in half.

Step 2. Fold and unfold in half both ways to form creased center lines. (Note: be sure paper is still folded in half.)

Step 3. Bring corner (1) right to meet the center line. Be sure to fold from the vertical crease line.

Step 4. Bring corner (1) left till edges coincide, then make the fold.

Step 5. Bring corner (2) left and fold.

Step 6. Bring corner (2) right until edges coincide. Then fold.

Step 7. Cut on the angle as shown in the picture. Then unfold the small piece.

Step 8. Marvel at your perfect (we hope!) 5-pointed star! If your star is not perfect, take a fresh piece of paper (8-1/2" x 10" -- not 8-1/2" x 11") and return to Step 1.

Cut a star with the snip.

Betsy Ross sewing the first flag in 1776. Copy of painting attributed to Frank McKernan.

had been widowed just the year before, so she was eager for any work. When Ross answered the men's knock, she smiled in greeting, recognizing her relative George Ross and George Washington, for whose family she had previously done some sewing.

The three men politely removed their broad-brimmed hats as she led them into her sunlit parlor with its six-over-nine paned window. After exchanging pleasantries, the men stated their business—they asked her to sew the flag for the new nation. "I've never made a flag before," she is said to have answered, "but I'll certainly try."

They then showed her a rough sketch of the Stars and Stripes, featuring six-pointed stars laid upon the blue field. She pointed out that it would be less trouble to use a five-pointed star. When Washington voiced his doubts, she took a sheet of paper, folded it seven times, and then made one cut with her scissors. When she unfolded the paper, a perfectly cut five-point star lay in her hand. The demonstration served to reassure the men that the work on the symbol of their nation was in good hands. Once the flag was completed, George Washington was said to be so pleased with her handiwork that he exhibited the flag to all in Congress. (See color insert.)

It's a wonderful story that people remember as one of the facts about our flag. But not everyone thinks this quaint scenario actually occurred. As the old saying goes, "Consider the source."

The first public rendition of the Betsy Ross story seems to have originated with Betsy's grandson, William J. Canby. In March of 1870, when he was forty-five years old, Canby read this account before the Pennsylvania Historical Society. He claimed that the story had been passed down through his family over the years.

Once a story like this catches on, nothing can stop it—not even the truth. *Harper's Monthly* featured it in its July 1873 issue; by the 1880s school textbooks were including it as historical fact. Thousands of people who attended the 1893 World's Columbian Exposition in Chicago gathered to view a painting by Charles H. Weisgerber titled *The Birth of Our Nation's Flag*—it depicted the young Betsy Ross, hard at work at her sewing. As much as this story remains embedded in the memories of most Americans, some historians doubt that it ever took place. They point out that the 1776 meeting with Betsy Ross was said to have occurred a full year prior to the date in 1777 when Congress resolved to create a national flag; therefore, where would the need be to talk to the young seamstress? Also, an exhaustive search of the *Journal* of the Congress turns up absolutely no mention of an assignment given to any of the three men in question. There are even some who suggest that Canby created the story out of whole cloth, simply to add some glamour to his rather pedestrian roots.

The Betsy-Ross-story believers—and there are many of them—fire back with persuasive arguments of their own. They point to sworn affidavits by Betsy's daughter and other descendants that support Canby's story. As to the absence of any congressional record of such a flag committee, the pro-Betsy faction claims that the *Journal* of the Congress was notoriously unreliable. Committees were being formed all the time and some of those were considered "secret." "Also," they argue, "why would Congress keep any record of three men simply meeting with a young seamstress to have a flag sewn?"

The "Anti-Betsy Group," as they're referred to by sworn Ross believers, ask why Congress would plan to replace the Grand Union flag, first flown in January of 1776, only six months later? Betsy supporters claim that Congress was dismayed by the reaction of the British to the Grand Union flag with the Union Jack in the canton—therefore, they were in a hurry to get a new flag produced. To support this argument they cite a 1784 painting by Charles Willson Peale entitled

So Many Stories, So Many Questions

As I conducted my research for this book, I came across hundreds of stories that at first glance seemed incredibly fascinating in their sense of drama and coincidence. I soon found that *incredible* was the right word to use for most of them, simply because they turned out to be false.

For example, consider the Schuyler flag. The background story seems perfectly reasonable. Philip Schuyler was a delegate from New York to the Continental Congress and was in Philadelphia in April of 1777. Schuyler had previously served in various military posts with the Continental Army and therefore had a real appreciation for flags and their role in battle. Once he heard that Betsy Ross had just finished making the new flag for America, he had to have one for himself. He hired Betsy to make him a flag just like her first.

The story goes on to state that this second flag was inherited by Schuyler's daughter, the wife of Alexander Hamilton, and was passed on from there down through the generations. It was finally donated by the family to the Fort Ticonderoga Museum in Ticonderoga, New York, and is on exhibit as the oldest American flag in existence (assuming the one made for Washington has disappeared over the years).

"What a story," I thought. "Here's the actual second U.S. flag ever made, and direct from the needle of Betsy Ross. This has to be a real plus for the pro-Betsy crowd."

I called the museum and spoke with its curator, a friendly fellow named Chris Fox, hoping to get a private showing of the flag. My hopes were soon dashed, however, when Chris told me that the Schuyler story was simply a myth—the absolute earliest date the flag could be traced to was sometime in the early nineteenth century.

Birth of Our Nation's Flag *painting by Charles H. Weisgerber.*

Washington at the Battle of Princeton. In this painting of a battle that took place in January of 1777, five months before the congressional flag resolution, Peale portrayed the American flag with a circle of thirteen white stars against a field of blue. This proves that Ross sewed the flag, argue her supporters somewhat disingenuously, because it shows that the Grand Union flag had ceased being carried before the resolution in June of that year. Of course, as the example of Mel Gibson's *The Patriot* showed, the media should not be relied upon as the final word in any historical debate—but Ross supporters correctly point out that Peale was noted for his fanatical devotion to historical accuracy in his paintings.

The *New Columbia Encyclopedia* states: "the long-accepted story that she [Betsy Ross] designed and made the first American national flag [the Stars and Stripes] is generally discredited." The word *generally* seems to me to be playing it safe by providing a qualifier. So until someone comes up with irrefutable proof one way or the other—and even then someone will refute it—the argument rages on.

SO WHAT *DO* WE KNOW ABOUT BETSY ROSS?

We do know that Betsy Ross was a seamstress who lived on Arch Street in Philadelphia. In fact, you can visit her charming Georgian-style house today, located at 239 Arch Street. It's even open to the public—more than two hundred and fifty thousand people visit it each year. Originally erected in 1740, it was acquired by the Betsy Ross Memorial Association in 1898 through the efforts of a massive fund drive. By selling "Betsy Ross Certificates" at a dime apiece to more than 2 million people, the group was able to restore the house and establish it as a national shrine. In 1937 the Betsy Ross Memorial Association donated the house to the city of Philadelphia. Betsy and her third husband, John Claypoole, are buried in the house's courtyard.

The only other relevant fact that can be proven is that in May of 1777, the government of the state of Pennsylvania asked Betsy Ross to sew flags for the Pennsylvanian Navy.

WHO IS FRANCIS HOPKINSON?

Francis Hopkinson, a senator from New Jersey and one of the signers of the Declaration of Independence, was also a man of letters and an accomplished artist. His design work includes the official seals for the state of New Jersey and the College of Philadelphia (now the University of Pennsylvania), as well as the Continental currency. He was also one of three commissioners of the early American Navy Board and was a judge of the Pennsylvania Admiralty Court.

On May 25, 1780, three years after Congress passed the Flag Resolution, Hopkinson wrote to the Board of Admiralty expressing his pleasure over their accepting a seal he had designed for them. In his letter he listed other work he had done, including "A Great Seal for the United States of America" and "The Flag of the United States of America." Hopkinson referred to these designs as "Labours of Fancy" and stated that although he made these designs free of charge, he would appreciate receiving a "Quarter cask of the public wine" from the government as a token of gratitude. Congress thought otherwise, however, and Hopkinson went thirsty.

He then submitted a formal bill to Congress for his designs in the amount of $2,700. That claim, like the request for the

The flag is raised for the first time outside the Continental Congress in Philadelphia. Painting by Charles H. Weisgerber.

A Statement by the Daughter of Betsy Ross

Rachel Fletcher was the daughter of Betsy Ross (later known as Elizabeth Claypoole). In 1871 Rachel made an affidavit in which she recalled her mother's words about making the American flag.

I remember having heard my mother Elizabeth Claypoole say frequently that she, with her own hands (while she was the widow of John Ross), made the first Star-spangled Banner that ever was made. I remember to have heard her also say that it was made on the order of a Committee, of whom Col. Ross was one, and that Robert Morris was also one of the Committee. That General Washington, acting in conference with the committee, called with them at her house. This house was on the north side of Arch Street a few doors below Third Street, above Bread Street, a two-story house, with attic and a dormer window, now standing, the only one of the row left, the old number being 89; it was formerly occupied by Daniel Niles, Shoemaker. Mother at first lived in the house next east, and when the war came, she moved into the house of Daniel Niles. That it was in the month of June 1776, or shortly before the Declaration of Independence that the committee called on her. That the member of the committee named Ross was an uncle of her deceased husband. That she was previously well acquainted with Washington, and that he had often been in her house in friendly visits, as well as on business. That she had embroidered ruffles for his shirt bosoms and cuffs, and that it was partly owing to his friendship for her that she was chosen to make the flag. That when the committee (with General Washington) came into her store she showed them into her parlor, back of her store; and one of them asked her if she could make a flag and that she replied that she did not know but she could try. That they then showed her a drawing roughly executed, of the flag as it was proposed to be made by the committee, and that she saw in it some defects in its proportions and the arrangement and shape of the stars. That she said it was square and a flag should be one third longer than its width, that the stars were scattered promiscuously over the field, and she said they should be either in lines or in some adopted form as a circle, or a star, and that the stars were six-pointed in the drawing, and she said they should be five pointed. That the gentlemen of the committee and General Washington very respectfully considered the suggestions and acted upon them, General Washington seating himself at a table with a pencil and paper, altered the drawing and then made a new one according to the suggestions of my mother. That General Washington seemed to her to be the active one in making the design, the others having little or nothing to do with it. That the committee then requested her to call on one of their number, a shipping merchant on the wharf, and then adjourned. That she was punctual to her appointment, and then the gentleman drew out of a chest an old ship's color which he loaned her to show her how the sewing was done; and also gave her the drawing finished according to her suggestions. That this drawing was done in water colors by William Barrett, an artist, who lived on the north side of Cherry Street above Third Street, a large three-story brick house on the west side of an alley which ran back to the Pennsylvania Academy for Young Ladies, kept by James A. Neal, the best school of the kind in the city at that time. That Barrett only did the painting, and had nothing to do with the design. He was often employed by mother afterwards to paint the coats of arms

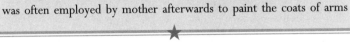

of the United States and of the States on silk flags. That other designs had also been made by the committee and given to other seamstresses to make, but that they were not approved. That mother went diligently to work upon her flag and soon finished it, and returned it, the first star-spangled banner that ever was made, to her employers, that it was run up to the peak of one of the vessels belonging to one of the committee then lying at the wharf, and was received with shouts of applause by the few bystanders who happened to be looking on. That the committee on the same day carried the flag into the Congress sitting in the State House, and made a report presenting the flag and the drawing and that Congress unanimously approved and accepted the report. That the next day Col. Ross called upon my mother and informed her that her work had been approved and her flag adopted, and he gave orders for the purchase of all the materials and the manufacture of as many flags as she could make. And that from that time forward, for over fifty years she continued to make flags for the United States government.

This statement was signed, affirmed, and subscribed to by Rachel Fletcher on July 31, 1871.

wine, was refused. Irate, Hopkinson resigned his post as Treasurer of Loans. At this point a congressional committee decided to examine his claim and establish the relative merits. Their finding read: "That the report relative to the fancywork of F. Hopkinson ought not to be acted upon."

Poor Francis Hopkinson. Not only did he not get his money or his wine, he didn't even receive an acknowledgment as the designer of the flag—if in fact he was.

SO WHO ACTUALLY DESIGNED THE FLAG?

At this point there is no real answer. Unless some previously overlooked evidence finally comes to light, we'll never actually know who designed the flag we salute today. Was it Betsy Ross? Or Francis Hopkinson? Or perhaps even some unsung hero who toiled behind the scenes?

In the end, however, does it really matter who designed the flag? The fact is, those who are truly responsible for our flag and what it stands for are those Americans who risked life and liberty to bring our country into existence . . . those servicemen and -women who fight for it in times of peril . . . and each and every person who keeps its vision as bright and vibrant as it was the day the needle was lifted from the fabric. These are the individuals who keep our national banner flying over the home of the brave and the land of the free.

CHAPTER THREE

Our Flag Grows Up

Resolved, that the flag of the United States be made of thirteen stripes, alternate red and white; that the Union be thirteen stars, white in a blue field, representing a new constellation.

*A*s reverberant as those words resound throughout our history, they say nothing about exactly how the various elements should be arranged. Where should the blue field be placed? Should the stripes be vertical or horizontal? Not surprisingly, our national banner underwent many dramatic changes before it became the fifty-star flag we salute today.

At times, the flag has even varied from that terse description handed down by the Continental Congress back in 1777. We know of one example of this because of a scrappy young American naval hero who refused to accept defeat in spite of overwhelming odds.

In 1779 John Paul Jones was serving as captain of a some-

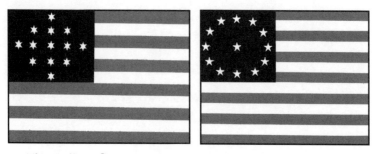

The Hulbert flag and the Third Maryland Regiment flag—
both are local variants.

what decrepit U.S. naval frigate christened the *Bon Homme Richard* (*The Good Man Richard*, named after Benjamin Franklin's alter ego, Poor Richard). On September 23, while in the waters of the North Sea, one of his crew called out that another ship was closing in on them. They soon found themselves confronted by the vastly superior British frigate *Serapis*. Jones quickly realized that his options were limited. The *Serapis* carried three times as many cannons as his ship, so a gun battle was futile. The British ship was also much faster than the *Bon Homme Richard,* so there was no chance of fleeing. There was only one thing left to do—Jones ordered his ship to sail head-on into the *Serapis*. When the two ships were actually touching, the Americans leaped to the deck of the British vessel carrying heavy ropes and lashed the two ships together. After three hours of brutal fighting, the captain of the *Serapis* saw that the American ship was beginning to sink due to the bursting of two of its cannons. He shouted a demand for Jones to surrender. Amid the clamor of the clashing swords and blasting pistols around him, the American commander glared up at his foe and responded with that challenge every schoolchild knows by heart: "Sir, I have not yet begun to fight!" A few minutes later he proved as good as his word when one of his crew lobbed a grenade into the munitions storage of the *Serapis*. The violent explosion crippled the ship and the British captain quickly offered his surrender. Jones and his crew then struck the colors on the *Bon Homme Richard* and quickly moved to the *Serapis*. Minutes later, the battered American vessel slipped beneath the waves.

A few days later, the *Serapis* and its new commander, John Paul Jones, limped into Texel, a harbor in neutral Holland. The Dutch authorities came aboard and Jones apprised them of the situation. However, when the local British ambassador was brought in, he demanded that they immediately seize the *Serapis* and imprison Jones and his crew. His reasoning? The flag that had flown from Jones's ship—and that his men had brought over to the British vessel—belonged to no recognized nation, he argued. Therefore, Jones and his crew were pirates, plain and simple.

The cautious Dutchmen, not wanting to get embroiled in an international dispute, decided to simply let both parties proceed on their way. However, not wanting to take any chances in case the situation came back to haunt them, they had an artist make a detailed painting of the flag the Ameri-

THE STARS AND STRIPES

With the Declaration of Independence from Great Britain in July of 1776, the young "United States of America" felt the need for a new, truly national flag. To fill this need Congress on 14 June 1777 resolved "that the flag of the United States be made of thirteen stripes, alternate red and white; that the union be thirteen stars, white in a blue field, representing a new constellation." Our new national flag was flown by John Paul Jones in February 1779, and it also flew over the American fortifications at Yorktown in 1781, when the combined American and French armies under Washington and Rochambeau defeated the British under Cornwallis.

The first Stars and Stripes

cans had saved from the *Bon Homme Richard.* (See color insert.) This painting, which now hangs in the Chicago Historical Society, is one of the first completely accurate portrayals of our nation's banner— and the flag it shows features thirteen stripes of red, white, and blue, in no particular order. Also, the thirteen stars had eight points each instead of the usual five.

Some historians believe that this flag had been designed by Benjamin Franklin—but like his nomination of the turkey as the national bird, the authorities ultimately chose someone else's design. Perhaps Jones found it fitting to fly Franklin's rejected flag from the mast of the ship that was also named after him. The one fact we're sure of, however, is that for the first hundred years of its existence, the American flag was of an eminently variable design. "Standardization is a modern concept that just didn't exist then," says noted John Paul Jones biographer William Gilkerson in his authoritative book *The Ships of John Paul Jones* (1987). "Modern historians are always looking for the quintessential item for a certain age— and there really isn't one."

"The Perfect Flag" by Hugh Downs

Hugh Downs is a television and radio commentator.

In my mind I have a standard of perfection for the flag of the United States: displayed on a flat surface the star field must, of course, be in the upper left; it must follow the design of being in what we in the television business call "aspect ratio" (wider than it is high in a 3:4 ratio); and the colors must be true—flat white and the primary colors of red and blue.

If fashioned of cloth and run up a flagpole, the pole or halyard end (star field) should be fortified by a narrow coarser white strip in which at least two grommets allow for threading of the halyard line. The pole height should be in proportion to the size of the flag. A small flag at the top of a very tall pole, or a short thin pole burdened with a very large flag, is offensive in my sight. Not so much because it is in bad taste but because if the flag is to represent our country, its appearance should mirror to a certain extent the balance, stability, grace, and beauty of the characteristics we salute in the nation, and the principles on which it was founded—which we are constantly striving to live up to. The "perfect" flag is then doing its job.

While proper reverence ought to be paid to this emblem, a fanatic fixation on flag etiquette can cause some people to confuse the symbol with the reality. Seeking to amend the Constitution to establish a law against burning the flag (a gesture of free speech) indicates a belief that the country represents the flag when it is actually the other way around. It shows a degree of confusion that is pathetic. When a flag has served its purpose and is worn out—in need of cleaning or mending, perhaps—the rule is not to clean or mend but to burn it. The fact that it is replaceable shows that it is not, in itself, the country it represents.

The perfect flag flies ahead of the nation, and this symbolism is capable of evoking a great deal of emotion. I often look at it and remind myself of the blessings I tend to take for granted. I can vote, I can say what I like without being arrested, I can pursue happiness—all of this because of the way this nation was put together. Seeing the flag as a symbol of this miracle brings tears to my eyes.

Another well-known example of this is the famed Star-Spangled Banner that inspired our national anthem when it flew over the embattled Fort McHenry in 1814. This enormous banner—thirty feet by forty-two feet—featured fifteen stripes, not the thirteen as specified in the Constitutional resolution. Was this just another case of lack of standardization? No, there was a method to this particular madness. By 1795 two more states—Kentucky and Vermont—had joined the Union. At this point Congress enacted a resolution called the Flag Law. It stated that for every new state, another star *and another stripe* would be added to the flag. Many senators felt that as our country grew in size, it was only appropriate that our flag should grow as well. The House of Representatives, however, were not so sanguine. One of the angriest representatives, Congressman Benjamin Goodhue, said, "If we con-

*Union soldiers of the Thirty-third Infantry with the flag
that accompanied them into battle.*

The second version of the Stars and Stripes—note the fifteen stripes.

tinue adding a star and a stripe each time a new state is admitted, the flag may have more stripes than a zebra and more stars than in the Heavens."

By 1817 five more states had been admitted to the Union—Tennessee, Ohio, Louisiana, Indiana, and Mississippi. It became apparent that the flag was soon going to get rather unwieldy. So on April 4, 1818, Congress passed a new resolution called the Flag Act, authored by Representative Peter H. Wendover in consultation with Captain Samuel Reid, a naval hero of the War of 1812. Wendover was one of the congressmen who disagreed with the Flag Law of 1795. In a report to Congress he wrote: "Should that practice (adding a stripe as well as a star) be followed, our flag would resemble nothing less than peppermint shirting."

Captain Reid is the one who suggested that the number of stripes be kept to thirteen to represent the thirteen original colonies. Adding a star for every new state would be an easier task, he pointed out.

The Flag Act stated: "That from and after the fourth day of July next, the Flag of the United States be thirteen horizontal stripes, alternate red and white; and the union have twenty stars, white in a blue field.

"That on the admission of every new State into the Union one star be added to the union of the flag; and that such addition shall take effect on the fourth of July next succeeding such admission."

Wendover was so excited that his recommendation had been signed into law that he immediately placed an order for a huge flag— twenty-seven feet by eighteen feet. Oddly enough, the seamstress who produced the flag was the wife of Captain Samuel Reid. This flag would be the first to

The third Stars and Stripes—note that even though there are now twenty stars, the number of stripes has been reduced to thirteen.

be produced in accordance with the Flag Act—with thirteen stripes and twenty stars. Wendover specified that the stars be arranged in the form of one large star. This flag was flown atop the Capitol dome.

Only a few months later, however, President Monroe added a codicil to the Flag Act that made Wendover's flag immediately obsolete. Monroe's addition stated that the twenty stars appear in four equal and parallel rows of five each. This

Weird States

The American flag may have undergone many changes over its lifetime, but the fact is that there could have been many more changes if some of the following odd states had stayed with us.

- Until 1796 there was a state called "Franklin," which is now part of the state of Tennessee.
- Other short-lived states include: Jefferson, Shasta, and Klamath (all in the territory around the border of Oregon and California); Superior (located in upper Michigan); and Nickajack (located in northern Alabama).
- By virtue of its state charter, Texas is allowed to divide itself into as many as five new states if it so wishes.
- West Virginia was originally established as the state of Kanawha.
- Utah was originally established as the state of Deseret.
- Delaware was originally part of the state of Pennsylvania.

was the first time that the arrangement of the stars in the flag had been spelled out.

Another milestone in the life of our flag occurred on March 17, 1824. On that date in Salem, Massachusetts, a young sea captain named William Driver was presented with a birthday gift by his mother and a group of Salem girls. Upon opening the package, he discovered they had given him a beautiful flag to fly from the mast of his ship. Driver was delighted and exclaimed, "I name her Old Glory!" And thus one of our flag's many sobriquets came to be.

Captain Driver quit the sea in 1837 and settled in Nashville, Tennessee. On patriotic days he would proudly display Old Glory strung from a rope that ran between his house and a tree across the street. After Tennessee seceded from the Union in 1861, Driver realized that his treasured possession was a likely target for vengeful Rebels, so he sewed Old Glory inside a comforter. When Union soldiers entered Nashville on February 25, 1862, Driver removed Old Glory from its hiding place and carried it to the state capitol building, where he raised it for all to see.

Union soldier carrying the flag and a satchel, ca. 1860.

Shortly before his death, the old sea captain placed a small bundle into the arms of his daughter. According to the legend, he said to her, "Mary Jane, this is my ship flag, Old Glory. It has been my constant companion. I love it as a mother loves her child. Cherish it as I have cherished it."

The flag remained a precious Driver family heirloom until 1922, at which time it was sent to the Smithsonian Institution

Happy Birthday, Dear Flag: The Story of Flag Day

Our nation did not officially begin to observe Flag Day until 108 years after Congress officially established our nation's flag.

It took some patriotic-minded citizens to bring it about. It began in 1885 with a public school teacher in the little town of Fredonia, Wisconsin. B. J. Cigrand had been teaching his class about how the flag was founded. He realized that there was no special day to commemorate the occasion, so he assembled his students together on June 14 to celebrate the "Flag's Birthday."

The Flag Day was a big hit, so Cigrand started to push to have it celebrated on a national level. He started to write magazine and newspaper articles and spoke to public groups.

A few years later another teacher, this one in New York City, began to celebrate the flag's anniversary as well. George Balch, a kindergarten teacher, worked up a special Flag Day observance ceremony. It was such a success that the New York State Board of Education decided to institute such a holiday throughout the state.

The Flag Day fever began to spread across the country. In June of 1901, the Betsy Ross House in Philadelphia started its own celebration, followed a year later by the New York Society of the Sons of the Revolution.

Then, in 1903, the government began to get in on the act, with the governors of Illinois and New York issuing executive orders directing that the flag be flown from all public buildings each June 14.

B. J. Cigrand continued his evangelism on behalf of the flag as he became one of the backers of the Prairie State's American Flag Day

Association. This group organized the observance of Flag Day in Chicago by setting up activities for almost three hundred thousand schoolchildren in five major city parks.

In 1914, as war clouds began to loom across the sea, Franklin E. Lane, U.S. secretary of the interior, delivered a Flag Day address to a receptive crowd in Washington. In his closing remarks, he spoke to the audience as if he were the flag itself addressing them, saying: "I am what you make me; nothing more. I swing before your eyes as a bright gleam of color, a symbol of yourselves."

Finally, the efforts of thousands of people across the country resulted in President Woodrow Wilson establishing June 14 of every year as the day on which the nation would observe Flag Day. However, he did not establish it as a national holiday; that happened thirty-three years later, when President Harry S Truman signed an Act of Congress establishing that fact.

B. J. Cigrand would have been proud.

Here are the words spoken by President Woodrow Wilson on Flag Day of 1917:

"This flag, which we honor and under which we serve, is the emblem of our unity, our power, our thought and purpose as a nation. It has no other character than that which we give it from generation to generation. The choices are ours. It floats in majestic silence above the hosts that execute those choices, whether in peace or in war. And yet, though silent, it speaks to us—speaks to us of the past, of the men and women who went before us, and of the records they wrote upon it.

> "We celebrate the day of its birth: and from its birth until now it has witnessed a great history, has floated on high the symbol of great events, of a great plan of life worked out by great people. . . .
>
> "Woe be to the man or group of men that seeks to stand in our way in this day of high resolution when every principle we hold dearest is to be vindicated and made secure for the salvation of the nation. We are ready to plead at the bar of history, and our flag shall wear a new luster. Once more we shall make good with our lives and fortunes the great faith to which we were born, and a new glory shall shine, in the face of our people."

in Washington, where it is carefully preserved under glass today.

In 1861, the United States suffered a grievous and fundamental challenge to the very principles upon which it had been founded only eighty-five years before. By this time the Union had grown to encompass thirty-three states. In January of 1861, after decades of social and economic conflict, seven southern states voted to secede from the Union, forming the Confederate States of America. Newly elected president Abraham Lincoln tried desperately to pull his country back together, but on April 12 of that year the Confederate Army commenced an attack on the federal forces in Fort Sumter, South Carolina. By the end of April, four more states joined the original seven in seceding from the Union. With the loss of these eleven states, our country had become a union of twenty-two states instead of thirty-three.

The question of how these events would affect the design of our nation's flag was surely not the most pressing issue of the day in light of the bloody battles taking place. But it was a real concern, given the flag's role as the vital and dominant symbol of the United States. Many of Lincoln's advisers maintained that he should remove eleven stars representing the seceded states from the field of blue. Popular sentiment among the people of the Union reflected this view. In fact, some residents of northern states had already started to display flags with eleven of the stars ripped off or defaced in some way.

It was a truly thorny situation that Lincoln wrestled with that April. Perhaps he recalled Benjamin Franklin's flag from the Revolutionary War days—the one that featured a snake cut into nine pieces, with the motto "Unite or Die."

He made his decision quickly. He announced that his mission as president was to preserve the Union at all costs. Therefore he would not allow the eleven stars to be stricken from the flag—to do so would be to acknowledge that the Union had actually been dismantled. It is perhaps ironic that the flag that was flown by Union troops throughout the long and bloody war carried the symbols of the states that were fighting them tooth and nail.

———

Confederate Flags

Although this book deals with the American flag, there's a fascinating story behind some of the flags adopted by the Confederate States of America.

The First National Flag of the Confederate States of America—also known as the Stars and Bars—flew from 1861 to 1863. Each of the seven stars represents a Confederate state as of March 1861, when the flag was adopted. Because of its similarity to the U.S. flag, difficulty arose in distinguishing one from the other, especially on the battlefield. This resulted in "friendly fire" and the capture of many prisoners of war on both sides.

The second Confederate flag.

The Second National Flag of the Confederacy was adopted on March 1, 1863, primarily to remove all similarities shared between the First National flag and the U.S. flag. This flag's long white field

The Confederate Navy Jack.

Four years later the battle was finally over and the Union remained unbroken. The United States not only retained its thirty-three states but over the next forty-seven years it would add fifteen more, bringing the total number of stars to forty-eight.

often made it look like a surrender flag in the midst of battle. It flew over Fort Sumter until the Confederate evacuation of Charleston in February of 1865.

The Third National Confederate flag was adopted by the Confederacy on March 4, 1865. It was designed to reduce the possibility of being mistaken for a surrender flag. For this purpose, a red stripe was added to the fly end of the flag. Today this stripe has come to symbolize the blood shed by Confederates during the war.

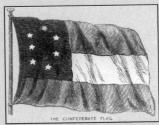

"The Confederate Flag."

The Confederate Navy Jack—known today by most as the Confederate flag—is the banner that many people expect to see flying over Fort Sumter. However, it never flew there or over any other official building of the Confederacy because it was not an official flag of the Confederate States of America. It was flown primarily on Confederate naval vessels. In spite of this, however, it has become the accepted Confederate flag, mostly because its dimensions are similar to those of the U.S. flag.

In 1912 New Mexico and Arizona joined the Union as the forty-seventh and forty-eighth states. As arrangements were being made to change the configuration of the stars yet again, it came to the attention of President Taft that there were more than sixty different sizes and proportions of flags being

The High School Sophomore Who Designed Our Flag

That's right, a seventeen-year-old high school student designed the flag that flies across our country today.

It all began on a Friday back in 1958 when Robert G. Heft's high school class was assigned a project. Each student was allowed to create his or her own project—they would be graded on creativity and originality.

While other students puzzled over what they would choose, Robert Heft knew immediately what he would do. Robert was an avid student of government and politics, and he knew that Alaska and Hawaii were being considered for admission to the Union. Given that the U.S. flag had not changed in design since 1912, Heft figured that a new design had not yet been configured.

Over the next weekend Heft took the family flag and cut it into pieces. He then spent more than twelve straight hours designing and sewing a new arrangement of stars. His goal was to incorporate the two additional stars so that the change in design would be almost unnoticeable. His final design featured fifty stars in five rows of six stars alternating with four rows of five stars.

When Heft's mother came into the room and saw their family flag in tatters, she was aghast—didn't her son know he was desecrating the flag? Later, after he had turned in his project, Heft found that his teacher, Stanley Pratt, shared his mother's opinion. "He gave me a B-minus. He said it lacked originality," said Heft. "He said anybody could make a flag."

However, Pratt added that he would improve Robert's grade if he could get the U.S. government to accept his design.

Fired up by the challenge, the young man carried his flag to his congressman, Representative Walter Moeller. Moeller then submitted the flag to the committee in Washington in charge of such things, and once Alaska and Hawaii were admitted, it was Heft's design that was chosen over thousands of others.

On July 4, 1960, amid the din of military bands, young Robert Heft stood at attention by the side of President Dwight D. Eisenhower and Congressman Moeller as he watched his handmade flag being raised over the U.S. Capitol dome.

Since then, that same flag has been flown over every state capitol building and over eighty-eight U.S. embassies. Heft has turned down any and all offers to purchase his original flag, even one for $350,000.

A former mayor of Napoleon, Ohio, Heft now works with youth in Saginaw, Michigan. He also travels extensively throughout the United States speaking to civic, community, and school groups about the American flag.

made. As a result, he issued an Executive Order on June 24, 1912, establishing the twelve specific sizes and proportions in which the flag could be made. It also provided for the arrangement of the stars in six horizontal rows of eight each, a single point of each star to be pointing directly up.

In just one hundred and thirty-five years our flag had undergone dozens of changes and had added thirty-five new stars. For the next forty-six years, however, the flag of the United

States remained as it was. In spite of the incredible turmoil of that time—two world wars, a devastating national depression, and the advent of the cold war—no new states were brought into the Union and therefore no design changes were needed.

In January of 1959, however, flag makers prepared to add a forty-ninth star when Alaska became a state. President Eisenhower then issued the first Executive Order regarding the flag since 1912—the order directed that the field of stars include seven rows of seven stars each, staggered horizontally and vertically. (See color insert.)

The ink had barely dried on the order, however, when he had to issue yet another. In August Hawaii joined the Union as our fiftieth state, and so Eisenhower directed that the new flag would feature nine rows of stars staggered horizontally and eleven rows of stars staggered vertically.

WHEN WILL OUR FLAG CHANGE AGAIN?

The American flag has been unchanged since August of 1959, and thanks to the efforts of Presidents Taft and Eisenhower, it retains the same basic design and proportions.

The one wild card, of course, is the possible addition of more stars if in fact more states are created. The likeliest candidate for statehood is the Commonwealth of Puerto Rico. Puerto Rico is a self-governing entity in association with the United States. Its people are citizens of the United States with all the rights and privileges that conveys—with two important exceptions. Puerto Ricans do not pay federal taxes, and they cannot vote in national elections.

There have been several efforts in the last few decades to make Puerto Rico a full state. However, in the last three votes on the issue in Puerto Rico, its citizens have resoundingly rejected statehood.

I am sure that someone, somewhere, has already created the designs for the American flag to include several more stars. Whether we will eventually use those designs is hardly a burning issue. We do know one thing for certain, however: America is a nation of incredible growth and opportunity—if the occasion arises, our flag will always have room for one more star.

★

Robert Heft

Robert Heft was the designer of America's fifty-star flag.

Old Glory is more than a piece of cloth. It represents the very fabric of America and all who believe in and enjoy our many freedoms. God has truly blessed our land and its people.

★

CHAPTER FOUR

"Oh-h, Say Can You See":
Our Nation's Anthem

*O*ur national anthem—a fixture of patriotic ceremonies, sporting events, and many other gatherings—might never have come into being were it not for a gang of small-town merrymakers back in the early nineteenth century.

The story starts in late August 1814, in the village of Upper Marlboro, Maryland, some seventeen miles from our nation's fledgling capital. The leaders of England, still smarting from their defeat at the hands of the ragtag colonists in what they called the War of Rebellion, had decided to renew the hostilities. The resulting conflict is now known as the War of 1812.

The battle still raged two years after it had begun, and the British had just dealt the United States a serious blow by burning the city of Washington to the ground. As the news

The Flag That Survived D-Day

The morning of June 6, 1944, a fleet of Allied warships appeared in the steel gray fog off Normandy Beach. Operation Overlord, the grand and top-secret invasion of the Allied forces, had begun.

While Hitler's forces were massed up near Calais, France, where Allied intelligence had fooled them into thinking the first invasions would occur, there were still thousands of Nazi soldiers' gun emplacements ranging along the beaches of Normandy.

The day before, as American fighters of the Sixth Naval Battalion prepared their ships, the king and queen of England paid a surprise morale-boosting visit. Someone in the royal party gave an American flag to a seventeen-year-old sailor named Clyde Whirty. As he attached the flag to the bulldozer he would use the next day to clear paths on Utah Beach, a friend of his warned him that the flag would certainly draw German fire. Whirty simply shrugged and said, "If they kill me, they won't kill someone else."

Early the next morning, the U.S. destroyer *Corry* pulled close to the shore of Utah Beach and prepared to turn sideways to serve as steady gun platforms for the shore bombardment. The German guns

traveled throughout the countryside, despair and anger rose high among the citizenry.

One steamy August night, the men of Upper Marlboro were drowning their sorrows in drink at the local tavern. No one knows how the rumor started, but somehow the men became convinced that a report had just arrived stating that the American army had crushed the British force in immediately opened fire on the ship in spite of the thick smoke screens being laid down by Allied planes. Amid the chaos of the haze and the whistling shells, the *Corry* struck a mine, and within eight minutes she began to break in half. The captain ordered all men to abandon ship; the 284 men jumped into the fifty-four-degree water where they stayed for two hours, struggling to keep warm while trying to dodge the shower of bullets and flak that rained incessantly.

As Lieutenant Paul Garray stroked through the water, he looked over his shoulder to see the great ship shuddering in its death throes. There, on the main deck now slowly dipping beneath the waves, he spied the American flag. Garray did not hesitate; he kicked around and headed back, risking death from the vortex of the suction of the sinking ship. He snatched the flag off the rail and swiftly swam back to safety.

The torn and tattered flag is now a treasured part of a collection of World War II artifacts. Each year a dwindling number of survivors gather to remember the day.

Two hundred and eighty-four men sailed on the *Corry* that morning; two hundred and sixty of them—and one flag—survived.

Washington in retribution for the act of arson. This was cause for a round of drinks in celebration, the men decided. Reports of the day record that the "copious libations" went on for hours, with toast after toast being raised to the victorious American forces. It seems that one of the most vocal of the townsmen was the elderly Dr. William Beanes, a beloved local physician.

"Oh-h, Say Can You See": Our Nation's Anthem

Late that same evening three weary British soldiers walked into town and decided to enjoy an ale at the local tavern. Their timing couldn't have been worse—they walked through the doors of the tavern just as the riotous celebration was reaching its zenith. The soldiers were immediately set upon by the townsmen and were dragged down the street to the local jail. At the head of the macabre parade was the elderly Dr. Beanes, shouting his support for the actions of his fellows.

The next day, when cooler if perhaps slightly achy heads prevailed, the British soldiers were released from jail. They immediately reported to their commanding officers of the British fleet stationed in Chesapeake Bay and told what had happened to them. The starring actor in their story was, of course, Dr. Beanes.

Within hours Dr. Beanes found himself chained in the brig of a frigate. Word spread that the beloved physician faced deportation or even the noose. A message was sent to a close friend of the elderly doctor—a Washington attorney named Francis Scott Key—requesting his help.

The thirty-five-year-old lawyer was faced with a difficult decision. Though he was an ardent American and despised the British for their burning of the Capitol and the White House, he also had a wife and six children who depended on him. Getting involved in a case like this would certainly take much of his time and, even worse, might result in his being taken prisoner by the British. But Key was a deeply religious man, known for ministering to prisoners and the sick and elderly. He once wrote in a letter to his children, "All one can do is to pray and strive to do everything right and shun everything wrong."

He decided to take the case.

On September 7, accompanied by Colonel John Skinner, a U.S. agent for prisoner transfer, Key made his way to the flagship of the British admiral, under the white flag of truce. At first his entreaties fell on deaf ears—Admiral Cochrane insisted that Dr. Beanes would receive a severe punishment for his insulting behavior toward the British Crown. But then Colonel Skinner unveiled his trump card—a bundle of letters from British soldiers, all testifying to the wonderful care they had received from Dr. Beanes and other Americans when wounded in battle and taken prisoner. Admiral Cochrane

---

How to Obtain a Burial Flag for a Veteran

Any honorably discharged veteran is entitled to a burial flag. The funeral director, as part of the services, will make the necessary arrangements for the family on behalf of the veteran. The flag may be used to cover the casket and it is presented to the family as a keepsake. The local office of the Department of Veterans' Affairs can also provide information on the procedure for obtaining a flag for a deceased veteran.

---

read each and every letter—finally, his heart touched by the sentiments expressed by his own countrymen, he announced that the good doctor would be released. However, he added, Beanes, Key, and Skinner would have to remain on board the frigate for at least a few more days. He offered no explanation for this odd stipulation and left the room while Key and Skinner spluttered in protest.

What Cochrane refused to explain—for obvious reasons—was that the British were close to executing their strategy for launching a surprise attack on Fort McHenry, which stood guard over the harbor of Baltimore. At the same time, a massive land assault would be commenced on the city itself. The British could risk no leaks to the Americans about this plan—and one never knew what Dr. Beanes might have overheard during his brief imprisonment.

The three Americans remained on board as unwilling guests of the British admiralty for six days. On the afternoon of September 12, just hours before the assault on Fort McHenry and Baltimore was scheduled to begin, Admiral Cochrane directed that Key, Beanes, and Skinner be placed on a small sloop that would be kept behind the British fleet, out of harm's way. However, this position offered a clear view of the battlements of Fort McHenry.

At 7 A.M. on the morning of September 13, 1814, the British bombardment began. The attacking frigates fired more than 1,500 bombshells that weighed as much as 220 pounds each and were designed to explode on impact. But some of the fuses were faulty, causing a number of bombs to explode in midair, resulting in spectacular but ultimately harmless fireworks. And from the prows of small boats especially constructed for this purpose, the British fired the new Congreve rockets that traced wobbly arcs of red flame across the sky. As day became dusk and then into night, the attack continued. Finally, around 9:00 P.M. the onslaught ceased and an eerie stillness pervaded the harbor. Amid the thick haze of smoke and the choking stench of sulfur that hung heavy in the air, the three Americans slumped in despair against the sides of the sloop. They assumed that the end of the attack had signaled the surrender of the American forces. Was their new country to return to British domination after only forty years or so of freedom?

But then, at around 1:00 A.M. on the morning of the fourteenth, they were aroused by the first few explosions from the renewed bombardment. Through the next few hours Key and his companions watched anxiously as each burst lit up the night sky—would the huge American flag flying over Fort McHenry still be there? But the flag showed its colors each time through the curtain of smoke and the "rockets' red glare"—the deck of their small boat shuddered as the massive "bombs burst(ing) in the air." But then, only an hour or so before sunrise, the firing ceased once again.

Then, as the first few rays of dawn began to lighten the

Bernie Kopel

Bernie Kopel starred in TV's The Love Boat.

In December of 1955 I was drafted into the navy in one of the first peacetime drafts. I don't like to talk about my heroism but—okay, you forced it out of me—I served valorously as a librarian at the Naval Air Station in Norfolk and then as a librarian aboard the battleship *USS Iowa*. The *Iowa* took me all through the Caribbean, South America, and the Mediterranean—a prelude to the luxurious life I led twenty years later aboard the *Pacific Princess* on TV's *The Love Boat*.

Every time our Stars and Stripes were hoisted, accompanied by the bugle call, I could never hold back the powerful emotions of pride and love for our great country, and my profound gratitude for having been born in this, our homeland, our United States.

I am a second-generation American. My father and his family made the perilous journey in steerage from the Ukraine in 1914, fleeing persecution to make a new life in this land of opportunity and freedom.

Our beautiful flag flies from a big eucalyptus tree in front of our home, a daily reminder of the never to be forgotten, never to be taken for granted, freedoms—as a symbol of the brave and selfless men and women who gave their lives so that we may continue to enjoy these freedoms. As my wife and I awaited the birth of our second son in this great country, our feelings about our flag have never been so powerful.

sky, Key peered through the gloom. There, still flying high, despite being tattered and scorched, riddled by their enemy's worst efforts, was the flag!

After more than twenty-five hours of almost continuous sea and land assault—and repelled at every step by the dogged American forces—the British leaders had finally called off the attack, realizing that the cost in ammunition and lives was proving too dear. They prepared to leave the harbor of Baltimore still safe in the hands of the United States.

His heart bursting with joy, Key was so inspired by the drama of the moment that he felt the need to write his thoughts down on the only paper at hand, a tattered envelope. As the sloop made its way to the Baltimore piers, the words flowed out of him, filling the scrap of paper both front and back. That evening, safe in his room at the Indian Queen Hotel, he transcribed his hurried scrawls and added more verses.

The next morning he met his brother-in-law, Judge J. H. Nicholson, for breakfast. After enthralling his relative with a dramatic retelling of the last few days, Key pulled out a sheet of paper and handed it to Nicholson. He said it was a poem he had finished the night before and wondered if his brother-in-law might like to read it. Nicholson was impressed with the poem—so impressed that he almost immediately had it printed up in handbill form and distributed around Baltimore under the title: "The Defence of Fort M'Henry."

The people of Baltimore loved Key's poem and on September 20, the newspaper *Baltimore Patriot* printed it. Within a few months word of the verses had spread as far as Georgia and New Hampshire, where it was reprinted in the local papers.

Added to the words of the song was a note reading: "Tune: Anacreon in Heaven," which is the tune of an eighteenth-century London social club song.

In October of that year, a Baltimore actor was the first to sing Key's song, now called "The Star-Spangled Banner," in a public performance. It became a popular song that was performed at political gatherings. It remained just one of a number of patriotic songs, however, until March 3, 1931, when it was finally adopted as our national anthem. It won this distinction in spite of competition from other beloved songs, including "America the Beautiful" and "Yankee Doodle."

The lyrics have undergone some changes over the years. Key himself wrote several slightly different variations of the lyrics and never established which was the "official" version.

THE STAR-SPANGLED BANNER

Oh, say can you see, by the dawn's early light,
What so proudly we hailed at the twilight's last gleaming?
Whose broad stripes and bright stars, through the perilous fight,
O'er the ramparts we watched, were so gallantly streaming?
And the rockets' red glare, the bombs bursting in air,

Gave proof through the night that our flag was still there.
O say, does that star-spangled banner yet wave
O'er the land of the free and the home of the brave?

On the shore, dimly seen through the mists of the deep,
Where the foe's haughty host in dread silence reposes,
What is that which the breeze, o'er the towering steep,
As it fitfully blows, now conceals, now discloses?
Now it catches the gleam of the morning's first beam,
In full glory reflected now shines on the stream:
'Tis the star-spangled banner! O long may it wave
O'er the land of the free and the home of the brave.

And where is that band who so vauntingly swore
That the havoc of war and the battle's confusion
A home and a country should leave us no more?
Their blood has wiped out their foul footstep's pollution.
No refuge could save the hireling and slave
From the terror of flight, or the gloom of the grave:
And the star-spangled banner in triumph doth wave
O'er the land of the free and the home of the brave.

Oh! thus be it ever, when freemen shall stand
Between their loved homes and the war's desolation!
Blest with victory and peace, may the heaven-rescued land
Praise the Power that hath made and preserved us a nation.
Then conquer we must, for our cause it is just,

And this be our motto:"In God is our trust."
And the star-spangled banner forever shall wave
O'er the land of the free and the home of the brave!

THE BANNER ITSELF

Of course the story of "The Star-Spangled Banner" is not complete without an account of the actual flag that inspired it.

In the summer of 1814, several months before the attack by the British, the commander of the star-shaped Fort McHenry, Major George Armistead, requisitioned a flag so big that "the British would have no trouble seeing it from a distance." Two officers, a commodore and a general, were sent to the Baltimore home of Mary Young Pickersgill, a "maker of colours," and commissioned the flag. Mary and her thirteen-year-old daughter Caroline, working in an upstairs front bedroom, used four hundred yards of best-quality wool bunting. They cut fifteen stars that measured two feet from point to point. Eight red and seven white stripes, each two feet wide, were cut. By August it was finished. It measured thirty by forty-two feet and cost General Armistead the princely sum of $405.90.

The flag was kept by the general and passed down through his family until they donated it to the Smithsonian in 1907. Today it is on display in the Museum of American History at the Smithsonian where it is sheltered from dust and ultraviolet rays by a plastic filter. It is exposed for view-

Oddities of the Banner

Before the passage of the various Flag Acts and Flag Laws and Executive Orders that standardized the appearance of our nation's flag, people were much more casual about adding ornaments to it. The original Star-Spangled Banner is no exception.

- *The Legend of the "B."* On one of the red stripes there is a large embroidered letter "B." It has not been removed over the years because it is the policy of the Smithsonian to preserve artifacts and not dismantle them. There is a legend that the embroidered patch was applied to cover up the autograph of none other than Major George Armistead.
- *Why the Banner Has Shrunk.* Certainly the fact that it withstood the attack of rockets and bombs for more than twenty-four hours accounts for some of the shrinkage in the Star-Spangled Banner. However, there is another reason as well. It seems that after the War of 1812, someone decided that it would be a great idea to cut off parts of the actual Banner and sell them as souvenirs. At least two strips were cut off and sold before saner heads prevailed and stopped the practice.
- *The Legend of the Inverted "V."* In any close-up photo of the flag one can see what appears to be an inverted letter "V" on the tenth stripe from the top. The debate arises when the meaning of this odd addition is discussed. Some vexillologists believe that the letter is simply a patch put on a tear in the flag. Other people believe that it is a symbol, perhaps, of a military unit. And finally, there are those who think that it is actually an incomplete letter "A" rather than an inverted letter "V"—and that it was added in honor of Major George Armistead, the commander of Fort McHenry.

ing for only a few moments each hour so as to preserve the fragile fibers.

The rigors of battle and the wear of the years caused the famous flag to decrease in size—it now measures twenty-eight by thirty-two feet. In 1998 the Smithsonian began a long-term conservation project for the flag, which had become even more soiled and weakened over time. Conservation efforts began in June 1999, starting with the removal of the linen support backing that was sewn into place in 1914 using 1.7 million stitches. Painstaking steps have been taken to preserve the flag, including pH readings to measure the levels of acid or base in the fabric, color readings to analyze dyes in the fabric, and fiber analysis through microscopic examination. A thorough vacuuming of all surfaces and large-format photographing of every section of the flag to benchmark its condition took place before any actual conservation measures were started.

STARS AND STRIPES FOREVER

Almost every American is familiar with the striding rhythms of John Philip Sousa's most famous march—perhaps as heard in the faltering notes of a grade-school band or the bright and brassy blare coming from the bandstand in a small town on a warm summer night. Few people, however, have any idea that this music was born in tragedy.

In 1896 Sousa was on an extended European tour with his

band. They were performing in Naples when a message arrived telling him that his longtime manager, David Blakely, had just dropped dead of a heart attack back in the United States. Sousa's shock at losing an old friend and business associate was magnified by his feelings of homesickness. We now pick up the story in Sousa's own words from his autobiography, *Marching Along*:

We sailed on the *Teutonic* for America the following Saturday. Here came one of the most vivid incidents of my career. As the vessel steamed out of the harbor I was pacing the deck, absorbed in thoughts of my manager's death and the many duties and decisions, which awaited me in New York. Suddenly, I began to sense the rhythmic beat of a band playing within my brain. It kept on ceaselessly playing, playing, playing, playing. Throughout the whole tense voyage, that imaginary band continued to unfold the same themes, echoing and re-echoing the most distinct melody. I did not transfer a note of that music on paper while I was on the steamer, but when we reached shore, I set down the measures that my brain-band had been playing for me, and not a note of it has ever been changed. The composition is known the world over as "The Stars and Stripes Forever" and is probably my most popular march.

Sousa was born in Washington, D.C., in 1854 of immigrant parents. At the age of thirteen, Sousa announced his

The Only Places Where You Can Legally Fly Old Glory All Night

Presidential proclamations and laws authorize the display of the flag twenty-four hours a day at the following places:

Fort McHenry National Monument and Historic Shrine, Baltimore, Maryland (Presidential Proclamation No. 2795, July 2, 1948).

Flag House Square, Albemarle and Pratt Streets, Baltimore, Maryland (Public Law 83-319, approved March 26, 1954).

United States Marine Corps Memorial (Iwo Jima), Arlington, Virginia (Presidential Proclamation No. 3418, June 12, 1961).

On the Green of the Town of Lexington, Massachusetts (Public Law 89-335, approved November 8, 1965).

The White House, Washington, D.C. (Presidential Proclamation No. 4000, September 4, 1970).

Washington Monument, Washington, D.C. (Presidential Proclamation No. 4064, July 6, 1971, effective July 4, 1971).

Fifty flags of the United States are displayed at the Washington Monument continuously. United States Customs Ports of Entry, which are continually open (Presidential Proclamation No. 4131, May 5, 1972).

Grounds of the National Memorial Arch in Valley Forge State Park, Valley Forge, Pennsylvania (Public Law 94-53, approved July 4, 1975).

plans to run away from home and join the circus. Instead, his father marched him over to the local U.S. Marine base and enlisted Sousa as an apprentice in the Corps musical program. In twelve years, Sousa had become the leader of the U.S. Marine Band. As bandmaster Sousa played for five U.S. presidents. He was a prolific writer, with more than a hundred marches, sixteen operas, and sixty-two songs to his credit, including "Semper Fidelis," the official march of the U.S. Marine Corps. World renowned as the "March King," Sousa was awarded the Victorian Order by King Edward VII.

It is amazing that the notes and words of such an intensely American song have proven so inspirational to people around the world. A woman from France told Sousa that when she listened to "The Stars and Stripes Forever," it sounded to her "like the American eagle shooting arrows into the Aurora Borealis."

Perhaps the most significant tribute to Sousa's influence on American culture occurred when "The Stars and Stripes Forever" was designated as the national march of the United States on December 10, 1987. A White House memorandum states that the march has become "an integral part of the celebration of American life." Only one other song is officially recognized by the U.S. government—our national anthem, "The Star-Spangled Banner."

In 1932, at the age of seventy-seven, John Philip Sousa died only minutes after stepping away from the stage where he had been rehearsing the Ringgold Band in Reading,

Robert D. Jornlin

Robert D. Jornlin was the captain of LST 325.

We were all ex-Navy veterans, 19 World War II, 8 Korean War, and myself, a Vietnam vet. In the winter of 2001, we were bringing back a ship we had all served on—a 1942 Landing Ship Tank (LST). We had to bring it back from Europe to the United States, but we were unable to get it registered. We were told that this ship filled with veterans could not fly the U.S. flag! We told them to get out of the way, and we flew the flag from the flag staff and on the mainmast from the yardarm as well. We had all served and fought for that flag and nobody was going to tell us not to fly it.

When we came into Mobile, Alabama, after having crossed the Atlantic Ocean in midwinter, having traveled 4,200 miles in 29 days with a crew of the average age of 72 in a 58-year-old ship, we got the greatest homecoming anyone could get. We never expected a greeting like we got. We were met by hundreds of small boats all flying the Stars and Stripes, with signs saying "Welcome home, vets, welcome home LST 325."

I am willing to fight and die for my flag. This is my country and the flag represents it. It means freedom, and it gives you rights that you would never have anywhere else. The flag should never be mistreated or allowed to be burned. It hurts me when our citizens do not stand up when the flag passes in a parade. I think of all it stands for, and of all those who have sacrificed to keep it flying high. I am happy when I have a chance to stand, full of the greatest pride, as that beautiful flag goes by.

Pennsylvania. The piece he had just finished conducting? "The Stars and Stripes Forever," of course.

Here are the words John Philip Sousa wrote for his resounding march:

THE STARS AND STRIPES FOREVER

Let martial note in triumph float
And liberty extend its mighty hand
A flag appears 'mid thunderous cheers,
The banner of the Western land.
The emblem of the brave and true
Its folds protect no tyrant crew;
The red and white and starry blue
Is freedom's shield and hope.
Other nations may deem their flags the best
And cheer them with fervid elation
But the flag of the North and South and West
Is the flag of flags, the flag of Freedom's nation.

Hurrah for the flag of the free!
May it wave as our standard forever,
The gem of the land and the sea,
The banner of the right.
Let despots remember the day
When our fathers with mighty endeavor
Proclaimed as they marched to the fray

That by their might and by their right
It waves forever.

Let eagle shriek from lofty peak
The never-ending watchword of our land;
Let summer breeze waft through the trees
The echo of the chorus grand.
Sing out for liberty and light,
Sing out for freedom and the right.
Sing out for Union and its might,
O patriotic sons.
Other nations may deem their flags the best
And cheer them with fervid elation,
But the flag of the North and South and West
Is the flag of flags, the flag of Freedom's nation.

Hurrah for the flag of the free.
May it wave as our standard forever
The gem of the land and the sea,
The banner of the right.
Let despots remember the day
When our fathers with might endeavor
Proclaimed as they marched to the fray,
That by their might and by their right
It waves forever.

CHAPTER FIVE

"I Pledge Allegiance to the Flag . . ."

ITS BIRTH WAS NOT SO SIMPLE . . .

It seems like only yesterday—a September morning in 1932, the warm breezes coming in through the window a tantalizing reminder that while summer vacation was over, summer itself was still around. My friends and I sat ramrod straight at our desks, trying to act like the mature fifth graders we had just become at the William Hatch Grammar School in Oak Park, Illinois. The classroom door swung open and in walked our teacher. When she reached her desk, she turned toward the far corner of the room where a faded flag on an old oak pole was standing. All twenty-eight of us scrambled to our feet at once and stood at attention while we copied our teacher's every move. As one, we placed our hands over our hearts and began to say those words that have echoed throughout classrooms across America for decades: "I pledge allegiance to the Flag of the United States of America . . ."

I didn't know it, but those words had been written a scant forty-two years earlier.

THE REAL STORY BEHIND THE PLEDGE

The history of the Pledge of Allegiance is far shorter than that of our American flag—although it has gone through several revisions over the years, like our flag, and it has been at the center of the firestorms of controversy as well, again like the flag.

The creation of an oath by which citizens would swear their allegiance to their country would have been an alien concept to the men who founded America back in 1776. Such an oath would have smacked of royalism to them; the only such passage prescribed in the Constitution was a short one made by a president at his inauguration.

It's perhaps ironic that the origins of the pledge can be found in a promotion campaign for *The Youth's Companion*, a magazine that featured uplifting, moralistic adventure stories for children. In 1888 the *Companion* launched a program of "advancing patriotism" by flying Old Glory over every schoolhouse. The plan worked well—within a few years the flag was being flown over all government buildings, not just schools.

The editors of the *Companion* saw another opportunity as the year 1892 approached—the 400th anniversary of Columbus's "discovery of America." They organized a committee of state educators to plan a National Public School Celebration for this event, with special exercises to be planned for every school. The chairman of this committee was an ordained Baptist minister, Francis M. Bellamy. Coincidentally, Bellamy was also one of the editors of *The Youth's Companion.*

The committee produced a twenty-three-word pledge of loyalty that was to be a part of the exercises for the event. The oath was titled: "The Youth's Companion Flag Pledge."

On October 19, 1892, schoolchildren in Chicago

Children at the P. K. Vonge Elementary School in Gainesville, Florida, recite the Pledge of Allegiance while saluting, 1942.

gathered to hear a special proclamation by President Benjamin Harrison, then in town for the dedication of the Columbian Exposition of 1892. Then a color guard brought in the flag and the children touched their fingers to their foreheads in a military salute as they said the words:

"I Pledge Allegiance to the Flag . . ."

Dr. Henry Heimlich

Henry Heimlich invented the Heimlich maneuver.

It was January of 1944. After taking a surgical internship, I had joined the U.S. Navy because I love salt water and ships. Little did I know that, in a typical Heimlich maneuver, I would end up in the Gobi Desert riding a horse.

SACO (pronounced "socko") stands for the Sino-American Cooperative Organization; it was established during World War II by President Franklin Delano Roosevelt and Generalissimo Chiang Kai-shek. A top-secret group, it was led by the joint command of a Chinese general and an American admiral. Their mission was to perform intelligence and guerrilla operations within the local populace of China. It became known as the "Rice Paddy Navy."

Within a week of being assigned to SACO, I arrived at my post in Inner Mongolia, China, on the outskirts of the Gobi Desert. There were only twelve Americans in our group; our code name became the Apostles. Given that we experienced the same weather that would hit the Pacific coast three weeks later, one of our most critical missions was to relay this intelligence to the U.S. Navy fleet in order to help them plan bombing raids and landings on enemy-occupied beaches. There were thousands of Japanese troops stationed only ten miles away from our small camp, so our clothing and equipment carried no military markings. The one thing I truly missed, however, was an American flag to hang somewhere in camp.

As the only medical doctor around, I tended to the injuries and illnesses of our small group of Americans as well as our fellow 250 Chinese guerrillas and, eventually, thousands of Chinese civilians. Despite the secrecy of our mission, our presence soon became known to a Chinese Nationalist general stationed only a few miles away. He implored me to help him train a medical corps for his army of over 100,000 men. Within a few months we were running the first Chinese army medical corps in the history of that country.

After months of constant work and severe weather, with the added burden of maintaining the secrecy of our mission, we finally received the first message on our radio telegraph that did not have to be put through the laborious decoding process: "It's over," is all it said—the brevity of the message signaled the end of the war in a particularly poignant eloquence . . . and so we began to get ready for the long trek back to Shanghai.

On December 10, 1945, I was on the last leg of my journey home, serving as a doctor on the hospital ship *U.S.S. Repose* on its way back to America. As I reached the top of the steep gangplank, I lay down my duffel bag and instinctively turned to the ship's stern to give the usual snap salute to the flag before boarding. As my right hand came to my forehead in that automatic gesture, I finally saw the American flag—what a beautiful sight! For all those months I had seen only the colors of the Chinese Nationalist flags. My hand stayed up in salute—I do not know for how long—and then I brought it down very slowly. I knew I was home.

Something to Remember

by Eleanor V. Sass, New York City

Whenever I see our national flag, bright against the summer sky, two things come into my mind: a memory and a question.

The memory goes back to a little ceremony that took place every Fourth of July around the flagpole in my grandparents' front yard on Long Island, when I was a little girl of five or six or so.

Their house was right across the street from ours, so at the crack of dawn I'd dress hurriedly and race over to ring their doorbell. Fortunately, Grandpa was an early riser. Out he'd come carrying the neatly folded flag over his arm. At the pole, he'd untie ropes and fumble with different catches and pulleys while I'd jump up and down, eager for what I considered the big moment.

Grandpa would give the rope a couple of test tugs. Then, with a nod in my direction, he'd begin to raise the flag.

I pledge allegiance to my flag and to the Republic for which it stands: one nation, indivisible, with liberty and justice for all.

Over the next few decades the saying of the pledge became an integral part of most schools' opening exercises. In 1910, New York state legislators voted to require the recitation of the pledge each school day, and other states soon followed.

One feature of the pledge that was not addressed in any

"Oh, Columbia, the gem of the ocean," I'd sing out in my high, piping child's voice, "the home of the brave and the free. . . ." Grandpa always joined in the chorus: "Three cheers for the red, white, and blue," while a warm breeze gently blew the flag, now flying high at the top of the pole.

After this Grandpa and I would go into his kitchen where we'd eat cereal smothered with blueberries and cream while he told me stories about life in his native Germany and how he came to the United States when he was a boy of 14. "I'm so grateful to God," Grandpa would say, "for the privilege of living in such a wonderful country. Always remember, Eleanor, how lucky you are."

So that's the memory. And the question? It's this: Does a person have to come from someplace else to appreciate—really appreciate—all that our country's flag stands for, all that it means?

I hope not. I pray not.

law was how the salute was to be performed. Although the original pledge sayers had used a military salute—a somewhat odd gesture for elementary school children—other schools adopted their own versions. In some towns, children held their right hand across their chest, palm downward—just as people today hold their hands over their hearts. Other schools had their students extend their right hands toward the flag in what would now be considered the Nazi salute—though to be fair, the gesture was already well known as the Roman salute and it was only later that Hitler co-opted it for

Children of families of Japanese ancestry recite the Pledge of Allegiance in a school in an internment camp.

his own. And some schools would use an odd combination of both salutes—children would give the military salute until the word *flag* was said, then they would fling their arms forward as if they were shouting, "Heil!"

The first hint of controversy began in 1917, when Francis Bellamy, no longer on the staff of *The Youth's Companion*, began to assert that he was in fact the author of the pledge. Not so, responded the magazine in a pamphlet published later that year—it was actually James Upham, a former employee of the publisher, who had written the words. Upham, however, had died in 1905 and therefore was not available to support the magazine's claim.

Amazingly, this battle continued for decades. It came to a head in 1931 when the *New York Times*, upon the occasion of Bellamy's death, published an obituary stating that he was the author of the pledge. Upham's relatives saw this and cried foul. The fighting only became more ugly as the years went on. Finally, in 1939, members of the United States Flag Association stated that their research proved that Bellamy was the true author.

Unfortunately, even this august organization could not lay the matter to rest—a self-appointed expert, Gridley Adams, countered that Upham had clearly dictated the words to Bellamy. He so besieged the *World Almanac* with letters to this effect that the publication finally cried "uncle" in 1950 and printed that Bellamy had written the pledge "at the suggestion" of Upham.

Gridley Adams had been associated with the pledge and the flag for many years prior to his entrance into the authorship debate. In 1923 he was chosen as permanent chairman of a new National Flag Code Committee, organized to settle once and for all how citizens should fly the flag.

Adams immediately proposed that the pledge become part and parcel of the Flag Code. In addition, he urged that the words *my flag* be dropped in favor of the words *the flag of the*

The American Creed

As the year 1918 began, the United States was wracked with dissension and turmoil. Young American men were being shipped off to serve in the war in Europe in ever increasing numbers. Citizens began to protest American involvement in "Europe's troubles" and the forced recruitment of soldiers under the Selective Service Act. By the summer the war had forced the government to take control of industry, railroads, and food and fuel production. Taxes were raised to fund the war, postal rates went up, and censorship of some mail was being officially conducted. In May Congress passed the Sedition Act, which allowed war and draft protesters to be jailed. More than two thousand Americans were already behind bars for interfering with the draft, including one former U.S. congressman.

In an attempt to bring the focus back on the good elements of our country, Henry Sterling Chapin, New York's commissioner of education, proposed that a national writing contest be held to establish a creed for all Americans. News of the contest quickly spread throughout the United States. By the time of the contest deadline, more than

United States. ("I didn't like a pledge that any Hottentot could subscribe to," he said.) He also sought to bring some uniformity to the salutes used during the pledge, recommending that civilians should place their right hand over their heart. His suggestions were immediately adopted as part of the Flag Code.

three thousand entries had been received. After carefully reading through each of these entries, the judges selected William Tyler Page's entry as "the best summary of the political faith of America."

Mr. Page was a descendant of President John Tyler and of John Page, who served in the House of Representatives from 1789 to 1797. William Tyler Page himself had also served in Congress—as a congressional page in 1881. His winning essay established the American Creed with the following words:

> I believe in the United States of America as a Government of the people by the people, for the people, whose just powers are derived from the consent of the governed; a democracy in a Republic; a sovereign Nation of many sovereign States; a perfect Union, one and inseparable; established upon those principles of freedom, equality, justice, and humanity for which American patriots sacrificed their lives and fortunes.
>
> I therefore believe it is my duty to my Country to love it; to support its Constitution; to obey its laws; to respect its flag; and to defend it against all enemies.

A year later Adams again offered a change to the wording of the pledge. He now proposed that the words *of America* be added after the phrase *the United States*. ("I thought people ought to be sure which united states they're talking about," Adams later explained.)

It wasn't until the advent of World War II that Congress

finally adopted the Flag Code, which included the official words to the Pledge of Allegiance:

> I pledge allegiance to the flag of the United States of America and to the republic for which it stands, one nation, indivisible, with liberty and justice for all.

Another element of the debate that was to surround the pledge involved schools' requiring pupils to recite it. A Pennsylvania couple, members of the Jehovah's Witnesses, brought a federal suit against their school district because having to salute the flag contradicted the biblical book of Exodus's injunction against servitude to any graven image; therefore, they contended, requiring the pledge and the salute unjustly infringed on their freedom of religion. This suit reached the U.S. Supreme Court but was ultimately rejected. Three years later, however, the Court reversed its ruling in another case and stated that no one can be compelled to recite the pledge or even stand while others recite it.

In 1953 the pledge was once again targeted for revision. Congressman Louis C. Rabaut of Michigan had received a letter from one of his constituents recommending that the words *under God* be added to the pledge—just as Lincoln had used them in the Gettysburg Address. Rabaut acted quickly and introduced a resolution in the House to amend the pledge. The majority of public opinion supported this change, espe-

The flag is hoisted aloft just after Armistice by the weary but happy soldiers of the 105th Field Artillery in Etraye, France, November 11, 1918.

cially in the fervent patriotic spirit resulting from the Korean War—though there were of course a few dissenters, including the Unitarian Ministers Association and the Freethinkers of America.

Still, Rabaut's resolution sat unpassed until the following February, when the Reverend George Docherty, pastor of the New York Avenue Presbyterian Church, gave a special Lincoln Day sermon attended by President Dwight D. Eisenhower: "There [is] something missing in the pledge, [something that is] the characteristic and definitive factor in the

American way of life. Indeed, apart from the mention of the phrase, 'the United States of America,' it could be the pledge of any republic. In fact, I could hear little Muscovites repeat a similar pledge to their hammer-and-sickle flag in Moscow . . ." (as printed in the Congressional Record).

Congress went on to pass the resolution and President Eisenhower signed the new version of the pledge into law on Flag Day of 1954. The pledge now read:

> I pledge allegiance to the flag of the United States of America, and to the republic for which it stands, one nation under God, indivisible, with liberty and justice for all.

In his enthusiasm, Congressman Rabaut went on to hire a songwriter to set the pledge to music. He also got the House to authorize printing more than three hundred thousand copies of the sheet music and arranged for the first musical rendition in 1955 by the Singing Sergeants.

Another firestorm about the pledge erupted in June of 2002. A federal appeals court ruled that reciting the Pledge of Allegiance in public schools is an unconstitutional "endorsement of religion" because of the addition of the phrase "under God" by Congress in 1954. A three-member panel of the Ninth Circuit Court of Appeals remanded the case to a lower court. If allowed to stand, the ruling would apply to schools in the nine states covered by the Ninth Circuit.

1. One of the many flags
of Spain from the early seventeenth
century.

2. The flag of France from the early
seventeenth century.

3. The British Union Jack.

4. The New England flag.

5. The Grand Union flag.

6. The flag supposedly designed
by Betsy Ross.

8. The forty-nine-star flag was in
existence for only a few months.

7. The "Texel" flag flown by John Paul
Jones on the Bon Homme Richard.

9. The "Brave Heart" ornament,
designed by Christopher Radko.

10. An astronaut salutes the American flag on the moon.

11. The Spirit of 76
*painting by Archibald
Willard.*

*12. The flag with
gold fringe.*

Cliff Robertson

Cliff Robertson is an Academy Award–winning actor.

On the morning of September 11, 2001, I was flying my Beech Baron from Long Island, New York, to California. At 7,000 feet I happened to look down toward lower Manhattan; I saw billows of black smoke pouring upward. At first I thought it was a simple fire . . . until I suddenly saw the second column of smoke. Within seconds air traffic control was on the radio, directing me to land at the airport near Allentown, Pennsylvania. Six other aircraft, large jets and small planes, were jockeying with me for landing. As soon as my plane rolled to a stop, I jumped out and ran into the terminal. There I joined the other pilots watching the televised carnage of the World Trade towers over which I had just flown. Given that all flights were grounded for the next few days, I stayed in a local motel. The owner made sure that the American flag was flying high in the courtyard day and night.

At this most traumatic time—and in the knowledge that our future would never be the same—I was both comforted and assured by the reminder that our flag was still there.

As of this writing no resolution has been reached on this ruling. However, the announcement of the finding caused cries of outrage across the country and the world. Outraged lawmakers in Congress—both Republicans and Democrats—blasted the ruling as "outrageous," "nuts," and "stupid." The U.S. Senate was so outraged by the decision that it passed a

Benjamin S. Carson, M.D.

Dr. Benjamin Carson is the director of pediatric neurosurgery at Johns Hopkins.

I do an extensive amount of traveling, including travel abroad, and I am always extremely anxious to return to the United States of America. Although it is not a perfect country, it is by far the best country in which to live—and anyone who doesn't believe that should try living somewhere else for a while. The flag represents our country, and I have always felt a great deal of reverence for it. When I was in the ROTC and had flag duty, we always took great pains to make sure that the flag did not touch the ground when it was being put up, taken down, or folded. We have an American flag on our dining room table at home and there is a flagpole in our yard, which proudly displays the emblem of our country. I challenge everyone who reads this to say the Pledge of Allegiance to our flag—not simply recite the words but think about what they mean and then, in fact, live by that pledge.

resolution 99–0 "expressing support for the Pledge of Allegiance" and asking Senate counsel to "seek to intervene in the case."

So I think back once more to that September day in Oak Park, when I recited the Pledge of Allegiance the first day of fifth grade. I wonder . . . had I known then that the pledge was

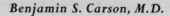

born out of a promotional campaign, or that it had caused such heated words in the highest levels of our government, or even were I to somehow learn of the controversies that might crop up in the future, would it have caused me to remove my hand from my heart and sit back in my seat? Would I have lost faith in my country—a country for which many of us in that classroom would go into battle on foreign soil only ten years later, so that someday our children would be able to stand in similar classrooms and make that same pledge?

I think not . . . I hope not.

CHAPTER SIX

The American Flag in Popular Culture

*H*oward Schnauber was just nineteen that day in 1941 when he went into the army recruiting office and asked what the army could do for a young man. The recruiter's reply was, "What can you do for the army?" Howard, a farm kid, didn't know the answer to that question, but the marine recruiter across the hall called him over. "I like your attitude," he said.

"Ten minutes later, I was in the Marine Corps." Harold laughed. When he was interviewed in 1994, half a century later, he was still proud of having been a marine.

Howard was born in Watertown, New York, and spent his first seven years in an orphanage, until he was farmed out to the Schnauber family who changed his name. He left them when he was just fourteen, striking out on his own, working on farms and for the Civilian Conservation Corps.

Howard went through boot camp at Parris Island and was

infused with the high standard for discipline necessary to the Corps. He was sent to New Zealand and then to the Guadalcanal Islands on August 7, 1942. Only two of the seven men he went in with survived. When he reached the beach, he dropped down behind a big coconut log and was able to silence the machine gun fire directed at the scene before him: a chaplain praying over a dead marine. Howard wondered how the sniper firing from a cave had missed hitting the minister. "I guess it kind of makes you believe in something more powerful than we are."

Mike Christian's Flag

Senator John McCain served as a navy pilot during the Vietnam War. He was shot down in 1967 and spent over five years as a prisoner of war.

The following is his tribute to a fellow prisoner and patriot, Mike Christian. He delivered these remarks at the 1988 Republican National Convention.

Let me tell you what I think about our Pledge for Allegiance, our flag, and our country. I want to tell you a story about when I was a prisoner of war. I spent five and a half years in the Hanoi Hilton. In the early years of our imprisonment, the North Vietnamese kept us in solitary confinement or two or three to a cell.

In 1971, the North Vietnamese moved us from these conditions of isolation into large rooms with as many as thirty to forty men to a room. This was, as you can imagine, a wonderful change. And was a direct result of the efforts of millions of Americans, led by people like Nancy and Ronald Reagan, on behalf of a few hundred POWs, 10,000 miles from home.

One of the men moved into my cell was Mike Christian. Mike came from a small town near Selma, Alabama. He didn't wear a pair of shoes until he was thirteen years old. At seventeen, he enlisted in the U.S. Navy. He later earned a commission. He became a naval flying officer and was shot down and captured in 1967. Mike had a keen and deep appreciation for the opportunities this country—and our military—provide for people who want to work and want to succeed.

The uniforms we wore in prison consisted of a blue short-sleeved shirt, trousers that looked like pajama trousers and rubber sandals that were made out of automobile tires. I recommend them highly; one pair lasted my entire stay.

As part of the change in treatment, the Vietnamese allowed some prisoners to receive packages from home. In some of these packages were handkerchiefs, scarves, and other items of clothing. Mike got himself a piece of white cloth and a piece of red cloth and fashioned himself a bamboo needle. Over a period of a couple of months, he sewed the American flag on the inside of his shirt.

Every afternoon, before we had a bowl of soup, we would hang Mike's shirt on the wall of our cell, and say the Pledge of Allegiance. I know that saying the Pledge of Allegiance may not seem the most important or meaningful part of our day now, but I can assure you that—for those men in that stark prison cell—it was indeed the most important and meaningful event of our day.

One day, the Vietnamese searched our cell and discovered Mike's shirt with the flag sewn inside, and removed it. That evening they returned, opened the door of the cell, called for Mike Christian to come out, closed the door of the cell, and for the benefit of all of us, beat Mike Christian severely for the next couple of hours.

Then they opened the door of the cell and threw him back inside. He was not in good shape. We tried to comfort and take care of him as well as we could. The cell in which we lived had a concrete slab in the middle on which we slept. Four naked light bulbs in each corner of the room.

After things quieted down, I went to lie down to go to sleep.

"That was my first experience as a young marine in combat. . . . We saw a lot of things that a human body shouldn't see—the type of things that stay with you the rest of your life . . . maybe God kind of messed up when he made the human body. Why didn't he put a device in there that would let you forget what happened fifty years ago? Today I don't even know what I did yesterday . . . but I can remember what happened. . . . These are the things that, in later years in life, come back to bother you."

Howard was wounded four times during World War II and

As I did, I happened to look in the corner of the room. Sitting there beneath that dim light bulb, with a piece of white cloth, a piece of red cloth, another shirt and his bamboo needle, was my friend, Mike Christian. Sitting there, with his eyes almost shut from his beating, making another American flag. He was not making the flag because it made Mike Christian feel better. He was making that flag because he knew how important it was for us to be able to pledge our allegiance to our flag and country.

Duty, Honor, Country. We must never forget those thousands of Americans who, with their courage, with their sacrifice, and with their lives, made those words live for all of us.

Mike Christian did survive his imprisonment, just like John McCain. He died in a house fire in 1983 at the age of forty-three.

once in Korea. He has scars and has had a knee replacement, but . . . "Nothing was so bad that I couldn't get over it."

Howard reflected on the many changes in society brought by World War II. "Things in 1945 and 1946 started to open up. People had a chance to go back to work. . . . It was different than before the war . . . it was the last of a depression; people had virtually nothing." Howard's adoptive family hadn't had electricity, but after the war because of the technology and companies getting back into business, everyone seemed to be lighthearted and happy. "It's amazing that we just seemed to like what we were doing. We enjoyed living and we showed it."

It was Howard's Korean war injury that brought him to Colorado for treatment at the VA hospital. Following treatment he worked for the State of Colorado for nineteen years. He was a park manager at Boyd Lake State Recreation Area and later with the Game and Fish Department. He was in charge of law enforcement and once again his marine training served him well—"you have to be firm, but you have to be just." Howard has been active in Veterans Service, helping to organize programs to provide transportation to the VA hospital. Another program serves homeless vets. Perhaps Howard's favorite role, however, is educating kids in respect for the American flag.

His poem, "My Name Is Old Glory," reflects a soldier's pride in his country's flag.

MY NAME IS OLD GLORY

Howard Schnauber

I am the flag of the United States of America.
My name is Old Glory.
I fly atop the world's tallest buildings.
I stand watch in America's halls of justice.
I fly majestically over great institutes of learning.
I stand guard with the greatest military power in the world.
Look up! And see me!

I stand for peace—honor—truth and justice.

I stand for freedom.

I am confident—I am arrogant

I am proud.

When I am flown with my fellow banners

My head is a little higher

My colors a little truer.

I bow to no one.

I am recognized all over the world.

I am worshiped—I am saluted—I am respected

I am revered—I am loved, and I am feared.

I have fought every battle of every war for more than 200 years:

Gettysburg, Shiloh, Appomattox, San Juan Hill, the trenches of
     France,

the Argonne Forest, Anzio, Rome, the beaches of Normandy,

the deserts of Africa, the cane fields of the Philippines, the rice
     paddies and jungles of

Guam, Okinawa, Japan, Korea, Vietnam, Guadalcanal,

New Britain, Peleliu, and many more islands.

And a score of places long forgotten by all but those who were
     with me.

I was there.

I led my soldiers—I followed them.

I watched over them.

They loved me.

I was on a small hill in Iwo Jima.

I was dirty, battle-worn and tired, but my soldiers cheered me, *and I was proud.*

I have been soiled, burned, torn and trampled on the streets of
countries I have helped set free.

It does not hurt, for I am invincible.

I have been soiled, burned, torn and trampled on the streets of
my country, and when it is by those
with whom I have served in battle—it hurts.

But I shall overcome—for I am strong.

I have slipped the bonds of Earth and stand watch over the
uncharted new frontiers of space
from my vantage point on the moon.

I have been a silent witness to all of America's finest hours.

But my finest hour comes when I am torn into strips to
be used for bandages for my wounded comrades on the field of
battle,

When I fly at half mast to honor my soldiers,

And when I lie in the trembling arms of a grieving
mother at the graveside of her fallen son.

I am proud.

My name is Old Glory.

Dear God—Long may I wave.

Joseph Rodman Drake was born in 1795 and died of con-
sumption at the age of twenty-five. He received his medical
degree in 1816 and wrote poetry in his spare time. On his

deathbed, he ordered his poems destroyed. Fortunately, his
daughter and his best friend, Fitz-Green Halleck, published
his poems; and Halleck wrote the last quatrain of "The American Flag," Drake's best-loved poem.

THE AMERICAN FLAG

Joseph Rodman Drake (1795–1820)

When Freedom from her mountain height
Unfurled her standard to the air,
She tore the azure robe of night,
And set the stars of glory there.
She mingled with its gorgeous dyes
The milky baldric of the skies,

And striped its pure celestial white
With streakings of the morning light;
Then from his mansion in the sun
She called her eagle bearer down,
And gave into his mighty hand
The symbol of her chosen land.

. . . .

Flag of the brave! thy folds shall fly,
The sign of hope and triumph high,
When speaks the signal trumpet tone,
And the long line comes gleaming on.
Ere yet the life-blood, warm and wet,
Has dimmed the glistening bayonet,
Each soldier eye shall brightly turn
To where thy sky-born glories burn,
And, as his springing steps advance,
Catch war and vengeance from the glance.
And when the cannon-mouthings loud
Heave in wild wreaths the battle shroud.
And gory sabres rise and fall
Like shoots of flame on midnight's pall;
Then shall thy meteor glances glow,
And cowering foes shall sink beneath
Each gallant arm that strikes below
That lovely messenger of death.

Flag of the seas! on ocean wave
Thy stars shall glitter o'er the brave;
When death, careering on the gale,
Sweeps darkly round the bellied sail,
And frighted waves rush wildly back
Before the broadside's reeling rack,
Each dying wanderer of the sea
Shall look at once to heaven and thee,
And smile to see thy splendors fly
In triumph o'er his closing eye.

Flag of the free heart's hope and home!
By angel hands to valor given;
Thy stars have lit the welkin dome,
And all thy hues were born in heaven.
Forever float that standard sheet!
Where breathes the foe but falls before us,
When Freedom's soil beneath our feet,
And Freedom's banner streaming o'er us?

And fixed as yonder orb divine.
That saw thy bannered blaze unfurled,
Shall thy proud stars resplendent shine,
The guard and glory of the world.

The Spirit of '76

Even though it was painted over 125 years ago and most people have no clue as to the artist's name, *The Spirit of '76* is still one of the most easily recognized paintings in this country. (See color insert.) Thousands of people each year visit the Town Hall of Marblehead, Massachusetts, where it now hangs. Perhaps the resolute determination so apparent in the faces of the young drummer boy, his elderly partner, and the bandaged fife player provide some comfort in a time of national stress.

Though the painting itself is well known, few are aware of the fascinating story that lies behind it. The artist was Archibald M. Willard, born in 1836 in Bedford, Ohio. Young Willard became an apprentice carriage painter and became well known for his distinctive ornamentation featuring landscapes and animals. After serving in the Union army during the Civil War, he began to paint humorous storytelling paintings of Americana, much like the work of Norman Rockwell. His first success was titled *Pluck,* a rollicking illustration featuring excited children holding on for dear life as the dog pulling their dogcart frantically chases a rabbit. Another more sober painting titled *Minute Men of the Revolution* showed a father and son leaving their home together for battle.

Willard's popularity was growing fast. He decided to produce something spectacular in honor of the upcoming American centennial in 1876. His first plan was to do another humorous painting called *Yankee Doodle,* showing a fife and drum band capering in riotous enthusiasm. After a few attempts, however, he realized that the centennial called for a work in a more serious vein.

He retained the idea of illustrating a fife and drum band, however. He turned to real life for his models: the forceful and determined old drummer was his father; the bandaged fifer was an old wartime buddy, Hugh Mosher; and the drummer boy was Harry Devereux, son of Civil War general J. H. Devereux. For the flag, Willard painted the ubiquitous "Betsy Ross" banner with its thirteen-star circle. Though debate still rages whether this flag ever really existed, Willard's painting further encouraged the belief that this was the "true" Revolutionary War banner.

The painting became a huge success. It was first exhibited in the window of a Cleveland art store, and the sidewalks were soon jammed with viewers. It then went on to its intended destination, the Centennial Exposition in Philadelphia; from there it traveled to Washington, Chicago, San Francisco, and many other cities.

The painting was finally purchased by the drummer boy's father, General Devereux; he then donated it to the town hall of his hometown, Marblehead, Massachusetts, where it soon picked up the nickname *The Spirit of '76*.

One newspaper reviewer noted: "It shows features which could be kind, but now are set like a flint in the face of the enemy. It is not the unreasoning courage of the professional soldier but the courage of men who have put character and thought and prayer into the music through which they utter their patriotic purpose. Those three men will stand and play until they die, or by their contagious heroism will turn the tide of battle.

Tom Day

Tom Day is the founder of Bugles Across America.

I have been a professional color guard marcher for over fifty years, so I guess you could say my life is about the flag and its display. I am also the Flag Protocol Advisor to the mayor of the city of Chicago. When I set up the display of flags that stand behind the mayor as he speaks, I always use some historic American flags from my own collection. To me, the American flag is a work of art.

A number of years ago, however, it became the wrong kind of art. The Art Institute of Chicago had brought in a new exhibit. In one piece, the artist had laid a large American flag on the floor and placed a "guestbook" at the top of the flag. Visitors were invited to sign the guestbook—but to get to it they would have to walk across the flag.

I was enraged when I heard about this, so I loaded my marching drum into my van, drove downtown to the Art Institute, parked on the sidewalk, and proceeded to march up and down Michigan Avenue while pounding on my drum. This caused a bit of a stir, to say the least, and soon local veterans and politicians were looking into the new exhibit. Before long, the flag and guestbook piece had been dismantled.

It is a free country, and you do have the right to do what you will to the flag.

Just don't do it around me.

Christopher Radko is a world-renowned designer of mouth-blown glass ornaments and holiday home decor. His career began in 1983 when his family's Christmas tree stand collapsed, shattering their collection of two thousand vintage European glass ornaments. Christopher suffered a double loss. Not only were the irreplaceable treasures gone, but with them vanished a tangible link to past holidays. Searching for replacements, he realized they were difficult to find, and he began a business that almost single-handedly revived the Eu-

Marine Private First Class Luther Leguire raises the U.S. flag at the American consulate in Seoul, Korea, while fighting for the city raged around the compound, September 27, 1950.

"The Star-Spangled Banner" Hits the Charts Once More

In late September of 2001, the music industry saw a massive surge in the sales of songs or artists who featured a patriotic element. Bruce Springsteen, Lee Greenwood, and even Kate Smith were among the top in-demand artists in the weeks following the terrorist attacks on our nation.

One of the hottest-selling singles had actually been recorded and released ten years earlier, when our country was in the middle of the Gulf War. Whitney Houston's performance of "The Star-Spangled Banner" was originally taped during Super Bowl XXV on January 27, 1991. In the days following the attacks on the World Trade Center and the Pentagon, Arista Records and Whitney Houston responded to the president's call for all Americans to proudly fly the American flag by immediately rereleasing the patriotic anthem to radio stations across the country.

The Arista label shipped over 750,000 copies of the single, which went on sale September 27 for $3.99. Both Whitney Houston and her label donated their royalties and net proceeds to the New York Fraternal Order of Police and the New York Firefighters 9/11 Disaster Relief Fund.

ropean tradition of mouth-blown, hand-painted glass ornaments. (See color insert.)

Here's what Christopher had to say about the Stars and Stripes in his essay "Flag":

The value and beauty of the American flag can be measured by the extent to which the ideals it represents are actively demonstrated not only at home, but also shared with people the world over.

Two U.S. officers plant the first flag on Guam eight minutes after the marines and army assault troops landed on the island on July 20, 1944.

As an artist, I see the colors of our flag aptly symbolizing the American theme of vast diversity coexisting in unity. In terms of graphic strength, the Stars and Stripes is a distinct and compelling emblem. The colors blue and red are at the opposite ends of the light spectrum, richly different from each other, and yet they work well together. The color white is created by combining all colors of light and appears on our flag in tandem with the red and blue as an illustration that opposites, and everything in between, can coexist in a unified form. As our currency states: E Pluribus Unum—from many, one. This is our strength as a nation, and a natural beacon to the multitudes that have arrived over the past two centuries and continue to arrive to call this land their new home.

Like the Statue of Liberty, Old Glory is for Americans a majestic and comforting sight announcing liberty, freedom, and opportunity.

Sixty years ago Franklin D. Roosevelt made a speech addressing our fundamental freedoms, freedoms that our flag calls for and guarantees. Many people know that these include freedoms of expression and worship, and freedom from want and fear, but few recall the truly revolutionary and heartfelt desire expressed on behalf of all Americans—namely that these go beyond self-interest. In Roosevelt's speech, time and time again he emphasized that these essential freedoms, which we seek to secure, are for the entire world and are to be enjoyed by people everywhere in all nations. Becoming American is not required or even necessary; these values transcend the borders of our land. They are bigger than any one country. Our flag represents these values for our country, but ultimately these freedoms are designed for all humankind.

Today, in the aftermath of September 11, our American flag endures as a silent and steadfast communicator to each of us as to the world. No matter what happens, our flag is still here, a rallying symbol reaffirming the principles of resilience, perseverance, inclusiveness, freedom, and a heartfelt connection with each other both in the heartland and the world over. Our unity as a people transcends our differences.

THE FLAG THAT'S NEVER FLOWN

David Fruge

In my Mother's house
The most prized possession is
The Flag that's never flown
It's never hung proudly
On the Fourth of July
To watch a marching band go by
It sits on the corner of a shelf
Standing there proudly
All by itself
Folded so neatly for all to see
I can never express how much
That Flag means to me
You see it's only been unfolded once
Then folded back up with care
After it honored the casket
Of the man whose name
I proudly wear.

Good-bye Dad.

In loving memory of my father, Chris Fruge, September 12, 1930–July 6, 1996, CW2
Christoval Fruge 16 Dec 68–22 Aug 69 9th Avn Bn—Dong Tam, Vietnam

The Flag of Iwo Jima

. . . so every son of a bitch on this whole cruddy island can see it!

The flag raising on Iwo Jima.

One of the most famous American flags is the one that was raised by six marines on February 23, 1945, on the embattled Pacific island of Iwo Jima. Four days earlier U.S. Marines had stormed the flanks of what the Japanese had considered their impregnable fortress—Mount Suribachi. The mountain was honeycombed with caves and tunnels that provided cover for a desperate Japanese army. Days of intense and bloody battle ensued, with both sides taking horrible casualties. At last, however, the maze of passages within and the craggy rocks above fell silent—the Americans had taken Mount Suribachi.

James Bradley, in his splendid book *Flags of Our Fathers*, tells the story of Iwo Jima and its famous image from a unique perspective—

his father, John "Doc" Bradley, was one of the six men raising the flag in the photograph.

Bradley relates how, after the mountain stronghold had finally been taken, forty marines crawled up the precipitous 550-foot sides while carrying a small American flag. Using pieces of pipe ripped from the fortress as a makeshift flagpole, they raised the American flag at the top at 10:20 A.M.—it was the first foreign flag to fly on Japanese soil. Thousands of marines and sailors cheered and naval ships offshore blared mighty blasts of their horns.

Perhaps because of the din, a small contingent of Japanese soldiers came racing out of hidden tunnels and another, smaller, firefight ensued, but the marines prevailed once more.

At this point an LST ship pulled up on the beach and a sergeant came running up to the group of marines. He was carrying a flag much larger than the one they had raised only a few hours before, measuring eight feet by almost five feet. The flag had originally flown on one of the ships that had been sunk in Pearl Harbor.

As he handed the flag over to the men, the sergeant said, "Colonel Johnson wants this big flag run up high so every son of a bitch on this whole cruddy island can see it!"

The six marines again made their way to the top and reenacted the flag raising. This time a few photographers captured the historic moment on film, including Joe Rosenthal, an Associated Press wire service photographer. It all happened so fast that he wasn't sure if he even got the picture.

Later, however, when the AP photo editor saw the print, he exclaimed, "Here's one for all time!"

The photo appeared in papers across America only two days later, on Sunday, February 25. The dramatic tension and the sense of victory against all odds the photo conveyed gave new hope to the American people, weary and discouraged after years of war.

Joe Rosenthal, a modest man, always took pains to point out that his photo was of the second raising, not the first. "Good luck was with me," he said, "that's all—the wind was rippling the flag right, the men in fine positions, and the day clear enough to bring everything into sharp focus."

Today, the very flag whose image atop Suribachi thrilled millions of Americans as they read their Sunday newspapers can be seen in the Marine Corps Museum in Washington, D.C.

I AM OLD GLORY

Master Sergeant Percy Webb, USMC

I Am Old Glory: For more than ten score years I have been the banner of hope and freedom for generation after generation of Americans.

Born amid the first flames of America's fight for freedom, I am the symbol of a country that has grown from a little group of thirteen colonies to a united nation of fifty sovereign states.

Planted firmly on the high pinnacle of American Faith my gently fluttering folds have proved an inspiration to untold millions.

Men have followed me into battle with unwavering courage. They have looked upon me as a symbol of national unity.

They have prayed that they and their fellow citizens might continue to enjoy the life, liberty and pursuit of happiness, which have been granted to every American as the heritage of free men.

So long as men love liberty more than life itself; so long as they treasure the priceless privileges bought with the blood of our forefathers; so long as the principles of truth, justice and charity for all remain deeply rooted in human hearts, I shall continue to be the enduring banner of the United States of America.

"It's a Grand Old Flag"

Another well-known song about our flag is "It's a Grand Old Flag," written by the famous Broadway producer and composer, George M. Cohan in 1905.

Cohan was "the original Yankee Doodle boy—born on the Fourth of July." Waving the American flag as a surefire finale to bring down the house with applause was established as authentic "theater" in Cohan shows. During World War I he wrote two of the most inspirational and popular American patriotic songs of the period: "It's a Grand Old Flag," which he wrote in 1905, and the stirring march, "Over There!" In 1936 he received a gold medal under a special act of Congress. The medal was presented to the actor at the White House by President Franklin D. Roosevelt, whom Mr. Cohan had impersonated in the musical comedy *I'd Rather Be Right*.

THE OLD FLAG

H. C. Bunner

Off with your hat as the flag goes by!
And let the heart have its say;
You're man enough for a tear in your eye
That you will never wipe away.
You're man enough for a thrill that goes
To your very finger-tips—
Ay! the lump just then in your throat that rose
Spoke more than your parted lips.
Lift up the boy on your shoulder high,
And show him the faded shred;
Those stripes would be red as the sunset sky
If death could have dyed them red.
Off with your hat as the flag goes by!
Uncover the youngster's head;
Teach him to hold it holy and high
For the sake of its sacred dead.

CHAPTER SEVEN

Amazing Flags, Stubborn Myths, and Incredible Facts

THE FLAG OF LIBERATION

Sunday, December 7, 1941. "A day that will live in infamy." On a quiet Sunday morning, Japanese fighter planes attacked the American naval base in Pearl Harbor, Hawaii. No warning had been given and as a result, the destruction and casualties were devastating. A total of 2,280 military men and women and 68 civilians were killed; 1,109 were wounded; and 19 naval vessels and 168 aircraft were completely destroyed.

The following morning, President Franklin D. Roosevelt issued an order directing that the American flag that had flown over the Capitol on December 7 be kept flying there— in spite of the fact that the flag is normally changed on a daily basis. Roosevelt then went to Congress and made the official request that we declare war on Japan and Germany.

I had served in the military during the last few months of World War II and had then returned to civilian life in 1946. At the end of 1950, however, I was called back into the service because of the Korean War.

I was sent to Fort Ord in California for a refresher course along with twelve other soldiers who had been called back. After a few weeks, we set sail for Korea aboard the *USS General Anderson* out of San Francisco.

It was the end of a beautiful day as we sailed under the Golden Gate Bridge and out of the harbor. There were several dozen of us sitting up on the top deck as the sun was setting in the western sky— as we looked back, we saw the bridge framed by Old Glory flying from the ship's flagpole. This was a wonderful and awesome sight, and I told my buddies, "Take a good long look at that, as some of us will never see it again."

We arrived in Korea in February of 1951. I volunteered to serve in my old outfit, the second Infantry Division, which was on the front

***

For three full days, as Congress drafted a suitable statement, that same flag flew above Washington—it was only lowered when the formal Declaration of War was finally issued.

Roosevelt then directed that the flag—which he now called the "Flag of Liberation"—be carefully preserved. The lines of the battle. Three months later, during a battle known as the May Massacre, I was taken prisoner by the enemy.

My friends, no one knows the trauma a soldier goes through when you're ordered to lay down your weapon and put up your hands. It is the worst thing I have ever had to do. You feel that you've let your family and your country down—and now you will end up a slave for the enemy.

For the next twenty-seven months I did not see the American flag. All I will say of that time is that life has a flavor that the protected will never know.

Finally, the war ended and we were exchanged for Korean POWs. The exchange happened at a place called Freedom Village. The very first thing I caught sight of as we were released was Old Glory flying high over the camp. What a wonderful sight!

Many people started to fly their flags after the tragedy of September 11—I've been flying mine for the past forty-nine years. It hurts me to see people at parades and other functions who don't show our flag the respect it deserves.

May God always bless America and long may Old Glory wave over the land of the free and the home of the brave.

folded banner accompanied him on many of his historic trips, including the voyage to French Morocco where he and British Prime Minister Winston Churchill met at the Casablanca Conference and announced their decision to join forces and fight the Axis powers.

On September 2, 1945, when two Japanese officials boarded the U.S. battleship *Missouri* to sign the official statement of surrender, the "Flag of Liberation" was flying high above them from the ship's mast.

An interesting side note: There was another flag flying over the *Missouri* that day—it was the American flag that had accompanied Commodore Matthew Perry in 1853 when he sailed into Tokyo Bay and thus opened Japan to commerce with the West for the first time. It had been flown to the *Missouri* from its home in the Naval Academy in Annapolis.

THE LINCOLN ASSASSINATION FLAGS

A shot rings out in a crowded theater . . . the assassin leaps from a balcony to the stage, his foot becoming entangled in a banner on the way and breaking his leg . . . a beloved president slumps in his chair, his lifeblood draining away.

Surviving that terrible night in 1865 is perhaps the most significant American flag in existence, second only to the Star-Spangled Banner. This flag, featuring thirty-six stars, has been authenticated by extensive research.

It must have been a chaotic and terrible few seconds for the people and players in Ford's Theatre that night. One moment they were comfortable in their seats watching a performance of the comedy *My American Cousin*—the next, a muffled pop was heard from the balcony, followed by a scream, a scuffle. A wild-eyed man leapt to the stage from above, yelling "Sic semper tyrannis" ("Thus always to tyrants") as he fell. He crumpled to the stage as his leg was broken by the impact, then rose shakily to his feet and ran through the darkened theater while people looked on in dazed confusion.

After a few moments, some of the players realized that whatever had happened had occurred up in the president's box, and they rushed up the narrow stairway and burst through the door. There they saw President Lincoln, slumped over in his chair, with a terrible wound visible in the back of his head. Laura Keene, one of the stars of the play, rushed over to Lincoln and cradled his head in her lap. Standing beside her were actress Jeannie Gourlay and her father, Thomas Gourlay, who did double duty as an actor and stage manager. Within a few minutes a doctor came rushing into the box and Gourlay helped get Lincoln's lanky frame stretched out onto the floor. Seeing that there was no cushion for the president's head, Gourlay pulled the large flag which had been draped over the balustrade and placed it partially under Lincoln's head.

After Lincoln was moved to Petersen House across the street from the theater, Gourlay took the flag, hid it, and kept it until, before his death in the 1880s, he gave it to his daughter, Jeannie Gourlay Struthers, who then passed on the flag to her son, V. Paul Struthers of Pike County, Pennsylvania. In 1954, Struthers donated the flag to the Pike County Historical Society. He also provided an oral history, which provided details of an unbroken chain of family ownership of the flag dating back to April 14, 1865.

Subsequently, the Society has had the flag's blood stains tested on two occasions. Both times, the tests confirmed that the stains on the flag are human blood. Further testing confirmed that the bloodstains are "contact stains," consistent with a bleeding wound coming into direct contact with the flag. These results, along with findings in other areas, such as the materials used in manufacture of the flag, the chain of custody of the flag, government policies on the use of American flags for ceremonial purposes, the disposition of all of the flags which were in Ford's Theatre on April 14, 1865, and so on, all help to confirm the fact that the "Lincoln flag" is authentic.

Today, Jeannie Gourlay Struthers rests peacefully in Milford Cemetery, her place in American history as an eyewitness to the assassination of Abraham Lincoln indelibly etched on the Ford's Theatre playbill for April 14, 1865. The flag, which she protected and preserved, is on permanent display at The Columns, the museum of the Pike County Historical Society.

THE OTHER FLAG IN FORD'S THEATRE

There was another flag in the presidential box that tragic evening; it hung to the left of Lincoln as he sat watching the play. Experts studying illustrations from that time period

Contrary to Popular Belief . . .

- . . . it is permitted to fly the American flag upside down—but only in an emergency. It means "Help me, I am in trouble!"
- . . . the American flag first flew over a foreign country in Libya, home of Muammar al-Qaddafi.
- . . . one does not have to destroy a flag if it touches the ground. The only rule in this regard is that the flag must remain suitable for display. The flag may in fact be washed or dry-cleaned to remain suitable for display.

★

have determined the six-foot silk flag's authenticity. Some of these drawings portray Lincoln grasping this flag after he was shot.

Now in possession of the Connecticut Historical Society, the flag had been originally taken from the theater by a Treasury Department official. It was later given to a Civil War veteran who passed it on to his son, a resident of Hartford, Connecticut. In 1922 the son donated it to the Historical Society where it ended up forgotten on a storage shelf.

In 1998, Kelly Nolin, a librarian at the Historical Society, was looking through the shelves for artifacts to use in a lecture on the Civil War. She spied an old mahogany box shoved toward the back of one shelf, and her curiosity piqued, she reached back and pulled it out. Brushing a thick film of dust from its glass lid, she saw a folded flag within, along with a plaque stating "Presented to Treasury Guard Regt. by the Ladies of the Treasury Dept. 1884." There were stories about a flag from Ford's Theatre being given to the Society many years before, but most people assumed they were just that— stories. When Nolin read the plaque, she said, "I just got real quiet, and my heart skipped a beat."

The flag is now in the collection of the Historical Society and is displayed at appropriate times throughout the year.

HANGED FOR TAKING DOWN A FLAG

Abraham Lincoln's first politically appointed general, Benjamin Franklin Butler, was sent to New Orleans in 1862 to oversee the Union occupation of the city. For the next eight months he ruled the city with such an iron hand that he became its most infamous and hated citizen.

The mood in the city was one of loathing—of the Union, the occupation, and the Yankee troops. Defiant New Orleanians weren't shy about expressing their feelings. Butler, in an attempt to quash any expression of anti-Union sentiment, cracked down on the citizens in a series of abhorrent actions. This earned him the nickname of "The Beast"—a title resonant among religious citizenry as the name of Satan's apocalyptic cohort, the Antichrist.

To demonstrate his intolerance for any signs of rebellion or hostility from among the populace of New Orleans, Butler had a New Orleanian—William Mumford—hanged for having the audacity to enter the New Orleans branch of the U.S. Mint and lower the American flag. As William Mumford's wife begged Butler to spare the life of her husband, Butler had him executed as an example of how he would treat all those who defied him in the least degree.

Although Butler quieted the gentlemen of New Orleans with Mumford's cold-blooded murder, New Orleans ladies of every social stratum were not deterred from expressing their contempt for Butler and his troops. Butler issued his infamous "Woman Order" on May 15, 1862. Modeled on similar orders issued in Maryland and Europe, the New Orleans "Woman Order" said:

General Benjamin Franklin Butler, aka "The Beast."

As the officers and soldiers of the United States have been subject to repeated insult from the women (calling themselves ladies) of New Orleans, in return for the most scrupulous non-interference and courtesy on our part, it is ordered that hereafter when any female shall, by word, gesture, or movement, insult or show contempt for any officer or soldier of the United States, she shall be regarded and held liable to be treated as a woman of the town plying her avocation.

In other words, a lady who failed to extend every courtesy and pleasantry to a federal soldier or officer was to be regarded and treated as a street prostitute.

After this, the only disrespect the women of New Orleans could show was to "inadvertently" empty their chamber pots and washbasins out their second-story windows onto the unsuspecting Yankees as they passed by on the sidewalk below.

THE LARGEST FLAG IN THE WORLD

While the late Thomas "Ski" Demski of Long Beach, California, was leafing through the *Guinness Book of World Records*, he read that the world's largest flag was one created for the People's Republic of China. "That really got my patriotic blood roiling," said Demski. "The world's largest flag has *got* to be an American flag." Demski had already commissioned a number of large flags through the years, including "Superflag I" (160 feet by 95 feet), which flew in Tampa, Florida, at Super Bowl XVIII in January 1984, so he knew where to turn. He called Humphrey's Flags of Pottstown, Pennsylvania, to make his world-record flag—and they did.

The flag measures 255 feet by 505 feet; it weighs 3,000 pounds. Each of its stars measures 17 feet across and the stripes are almost 20 feet in width. It travels in its own motor home, touring the country on display to marveling Americans everywhere. It has been hung from the top of the Hoover Dam and from the Washington Monument. And of course, it made the *Guinness Book of World Records.*

THE SMALLEST FLAG IN THE WORLD

The smallest American flag cannot be seen by the naked eye. It is found on a computer chip made by the Integrated Device Technology company. It measures only five microns in size.

THE HIGHEST AND DEEPEST FLAGS

Most people know that the highest point at which the American flag has been flown is on the surface of the moon, placed there by the *Apollo 11* astronauts in 1969. (See color insert.) This flag still flies where it was placed, and it will for centuries longer (unless someone else comes along and moves it). The airless environment of the moon guarantees that the fibers of the flag will not decay over time—but it also guarantees that there won't be any gusts of wind to billow it, so wires were sewn into the flag to keep it standing out from the pole.

Few, however, would know where our flag could be found in the deepest spot on Earth. It lies, seven miles below the surface of the Pacific Ocean, at the bottom of the Mariana Trench, 210 miles southwest of Guam. Two brave men, U.S. Navy Lieutenant Don Walsh and Swiss scientist Jacques Picard, descended to record depths in the bathyscaphe *Trieste* in January of 1960. Not only did the two men prove man's ability to design a craft able to withstand hundreds of thousands of pounds of deep-sea pressure, they also left an American flag on the historic spot. It was released in a weighted plastic container where it is most likely curiously regarded by the creatures that inhabit this dark and mysterious place.

THE FOLDING OF THE AMERICAN FLAG

As an army and navy custom, the American flag is lowered daily at the last note of "Taps." Special care should be taken that no part of the flag touches the ground. The flag is then carefully folded into the shape of a tricornered hat, emblematic of the hats worn by colonial soldiers during the War for

Independence. In the folding, the red and white stripes are finally wrapped into the blue, as the light of day vanishes into the darkness of night.

This custom of special folding is reserved for the U.S. flag alone.

THE FLAG FOLDING CEREMONY

The flag folding ceremony is a dramatic and uplifting way to honor the flag on special days, like Memorial Day or Veterans Day.

(Begin reading as Honor Guard or Flag Detail is coming forward.)

The flag folding ceremony represents the same religious principles on which our country was originally founded. The portion of the flag denoting honor is the canton of blue containing the stars representing the states our veterans served in uniform. The canton field of blue dresses from left to right and is inverted when draped as a pall on a casket of a veteran who has served our country in uniform.

In the Armed Forces of the United States, at the ceremony of retreat the flag is lowered, folded in a triangle fold and kept under watch throughout the night as a tribute to our nation's honored dead. The next morning it is brought

How to Fold the Flag

Step 1

To properly fold the
flag, begin by holding it
waist-high with another
person so that its surface
is parallel to the ground.

Step 2

Fold the lower half of
the stripe section length-
wise *over* the field of
stars, holding the bottom
and top edges securely.

Step 3

Fold the flag *again* length-
wise with the blue field
on the *outside*.

Step 4

Make a triangular fold
by bringing the striped
corner of the folded edge
to meet the open (top)
edge of the flag.

Step 5

Turn the outer (end) point inward, parallel to the open edge, to form a second triangle.

Step 6

The triangular folding is continued until the entire length of the flag is folded in this manner.

Step 7

When the flag is completely folded, only a triangular blue field of stars should be visible.

out and, at the ceremony of reveille, run aloft as a symbol of our belief in the resurrection of the body.

(*Wait for the Honor Guard or Flag Detail to unravel and fold the flag into a quarter fold—resume reading when Honor Guard is standing ready.*)

The first fold of our flag is a symbol of life.

The second fold is a symbol of our belief in the eternal life.

The third fold is made in honor and remembrance of the veteran departing our ranks who gave a portion of life for

Members of the "Old Guard" fold the U.S. flag during the retreat ceremony at the Arlington National Cemetery, 1968.

the defense of our country to attain a peace throughout the world.

The fourth fold represents our weaker nature, for as American citizens trusting in God, it is to Him we turn in times of peace as well as in times of war for His divine guidance.

The fifth fold is a tribute to our country, for in the words of Stephen Decatur, "Our country, in dealing with other countries, may she always be right; but it is still our country, right or wrong."

The sixth fold is for where our hearts lie. It is with our

heart that we pledge allegiance to the flag of the United States of America, and to the republic for which it stands, one nation, under God, indivisible, with liberty and justice for all.

The seventh fold is a tribute to our Armed Forces, for it is through the Armed Forces that we protect our country and our flag against all her enemies, whether they be found within or without the boundaries of our republic.

The eighth fold is a tribute to the one who entered in to the valley of the shadow of death, that we might see the light of day, and to honor mother, for whom it flies on mother's day.

The ninth fold is a tribute to womanhood; for it has been through their faith, love, loyalty and devotion that the character of the men and women who have made this country great have been molded.

The tenth fold is a tribute to father, for he, too, has given his sons and daughters for the defense of our country since they were first born.

The eleventh fold, in the eyes of a Hebrew citizen, represents the lower portion of the seal of King David and King Solomon, and glorifies, in their eyes, the God of Abraham, Isaac, and Jacob.

The twelfth fold, in the eyes of a Christian citizen, represents an emblem of eternity and glorifies, in their eyes, God the Father, the Son, and Holy Ghost.

When the flag is completely folded, the stars are uppermost, reminding us of our national motto, "In God We Trust."

(Wait for the Honor Guard or Flag Detail to inspect the flag—after the inspection, resume reading.)

After the flag is completely folded and tucked in, it takes on the appearance of a cocked hat, ever reminding us of the soldiers who served under General George Washington and the sailors and marines who served under Captain John Paul Jones who were followed by their comrades and shipmates in the Armed Forces of the United States, preserving for us the rights, privileges, and freedoms we enjoy today.

THE RAREST AMERICAN FLAG

The rarest American flag was the result of a flag manufacturer trying to beat the clock on admission of states to the Union.

Back in 1889, when our country was still in the process of adding states to our flag, many people believed that the two Dakotas (North and South) would be admitted to the Union as one state. One flag company decided that if they were to produce their flags early, they would have them available before any of the competition, so they went ahead and manufactured hundreds of thirty-nine-star flags. Unfortunately, they were wrong. When Congress admitted the Dakota territory that year, they divided it into two states—they also admitted Montana, Washington, and Idaho as well.

Today these thirty-nine-star flags are very rare, bringing amazingly high prices whenever the few that survive come up for sale.

COLLECTIBLE FLAGS

American flags are soaring in popularity as collectibles, according to Whitney Smith, director of the Flag Research Center in Winchester, Massachusetts. Smith says that the flag is an inordinately powerful artifact. "People fight and die over flags," he said in a recently published interview. "They provoke strong emotions."

Smith consulted on the largest flag auction ever, held at Sotheby's in May 2002. Response to the announcement of the auction resulted in a deluge of phone calls to Sotheby's from people expressing interest in attending or bidding by phone. "This particular flag fervor is certainly increased by the events of September 11," said Nancy Druckman, Sotheby's director of American folk art, "but interest in flags has been gathering momentum over the past decade."

The most sought-after American flags are those made before 1912, when the design and arrangement of flags was not dictated by legislation. In some flags from this period, the stars would form various patterns, such as a zigzag or spiral formation. Others featured different shades of blue and red. Experts say that flags from this preregulation era can sell for as much as $40,000. The same flags were selling for a tenth of that amount back in the early 1980s.

BE CAREFUL WHEN YOU COLLECT FLAGS

There are many things to keep in mind when you begin your collection of American flags. Jeff Bridgman of Jeff R. Bridgman American Antiques in York County, Pennsylvania, offers the following tips.

Unless you are buying from a dealer who knows a lot about flags, start small and be cautious. Most people, including almost all antiques dealers, know astonishingly little about early American flags. Be extremely wary of Internet auctions, take everything you hear with a grain of salt, and ask a lot of questions.

Know the two basic types of early flags: sewn flags and parade flags. Sewn flags are constructed by machine sewing, hand sewing, or by a combination of both, and were intended for long-term use. Parade flags are printed on cotton, silk, or wool. They were intended for short-term use at parades, political rallies, and other events. Both types are highly sought after by collectors for different reasons.

If you desire a sewn flag, buying big will sometimes save you money. In 1777 our flag was first used on ships, and this remained its primary use for the next hundred years. Most sewn flags of the nineteenth century are thus longer than eight feet, and simply too large for most people who wish to display them. This places a premium on small, early sewn flags. Making room for a large flag will often get you a more interesting example for less money.

Become aware of flag construction methods. For example, if a flag has machine sewing, it could not have been made earlier than the mid-1830s and was likely made no earlier than 1850. The treadle sewing machine was patented in the early 1840s, but it was not in widespread use until Singer marketed it in the mid-1850s. At least some treadle sewing seems to be present in 50 percent or more of Civil War–period flags. By the centennial it was used on almost all stripes, although stars were often still hand-appliquéd. By the turn of the twentieth century, hand sewing of American national flags had all but disappeared entirely, and zigzag machine stitching was first seen in flag manufacturing.

Life would be so uninteresting if we didn't have urban legends to spice things up and get people het up over nothing. Here are a few recent legends having to do with our flag.

Claim: ABC News asked their reporters not to wear American flag lapel pins or red, white, and blue ribbons in the aftermath of 9/11.

TRUE Since the September 11 terrorist attacks on the USA, many news outlets have asked or ordered their on-air personnel not to wear American flag lapel pins; red, white, and blue ribbons; or other patriotic symbols in order to "maintain an image of impartial neutrality" and to lessen the chances that overseas reporters could be harmed by those who might view them as an arm of the American government. Prominent among these outlets is the ABC network.

Claim: During a trip to China and Vietnam, President Clinton forced the captain of the U.S. Navy ship on which he was traveling

★

Don't get hung up on condition. Unlike samplers and quilts, most flags are expected to have been used outdoors. This often subjected them to wind and water damage despite the preservation efforts of their owners. Military use introduced other hazards and was generally more strenuous. For these reasons, flags are not expected to be perfect. Oftentimes they have the rips, tears, stains, and foxing that reveals to alter long-standing naval regulations and allow the American flag to fly below that of the flag of Vietnam.

FALSE Even though this report (which stemmed from a single Internet news source) flourished, Clinton actually traveled to Vietnam by air, not by ship.

Claim: A new can design introduced by Dr Pepper includes the text of the Pledge of Allegiance with the words "under God" omitted.

NOT QUITE In mid-November of 2001, Dr Pepper introduced a new can design featuring the Statue of Liberty with the words "One Nation . . . Indivisible" on the can. Even though only three of the thirty-one words from the pledge were used, critics and media outlets maintained that Dr Pepper had purposefully omitted "Under God" from the can.

their age. For many collectors, this adds significantly to their appeal, because history is apparent in the worn, weathered, and much loved symbol of our nation. Although condition plays some role in the price of an antique flag, it is far from the most important factor.

Conserve your flag properly. It is recommended that a flag be stitched to 100 percent cotton fabric or 100 percent cotton rag mat board. Of course, knowledge of the proper techniques is essential, and the flag should be covered, if possible, by glass or Plexiglas.

ARE THERE REALLY TWO AMERICAN FLAGS?

A pernicious rumor flying around the Internet states that the people of the United States actually have two national flags: one for our military government and another for the civil. The story goes on to say that the Stars and Stripes was actually meant to be used for military affairs only and that there is another flag with vertical stripes, which was meant to be used in peacetime.

It seems that this rumor got its start from a novel written long before the Internet reared its ugly head: Nathaniel Hawthorne's *The Scarlet Letter,* published in 1850. The introduction in the second edition, titled "The Custom House," includes this description:

> From the loftiest point of its roof, during precisely three and a half hours of each forenoon, floats or droops, in breeze or calm, the banner of the republic; but with the thirteen stripes turned vertically, instead of horizontally, and thus indicating that a civil, and not a military post of Uncle Sam's government, is here established.

The reason for this insistence on the two American flags? It seems that the people behind this believe that the United States has been under illegal martial law since the Civil War. Therefore, the government flies only the wartime flag (our Star-Spangled Banner) rather than the peacetime flag that Hawthorne describes. This reasoning seems to be an integral part of the rhetoric of many of the militia groups that have shown up around our country—groups that have a stake in claiming that our government is not in fact a legitimate entity.

Before anyone becomes alarmed, let me lay this matter to rest. The banner described by Hawthorne is in fact the flag that is authorized to fly from each and every Custom House, the U.S. Customs Ensign. This flag features vertical stripes and is still used today by the Coast Guard (with the addition of the USCG seal in the center of the fly). Rest assured that ever since 1777, the only official U.S. flag for civilian or military or any other use has been the Stars and Stripes.

WHAT DIFFERENCE DOES THE GOLD FRINGE MAKE?

I'm sure most of us remember seeing a flag with gold trim or tassels sewn to the three free edges. Perhaps it was on the stage of your grammar school auditorium, or maybe in the corner of the city clerk's office where you went to pay your overdue parking tickets. But what does the gold fringe *mean*, if anything? After researching this question via literally hundreds of reputable sources, I've come to this simple answer: It looks nice. Tradition holds that the fringe is used on flags displayed indoors only, probably because wet tassels would look ugly. (See color insert.) In the book *So Proudly We Hail: The History of the United States Flag,* authors William R. Furlong and Byron McCandless state: "The placing of a fringe on Our Flag is optional with the person of organization, and no Act of Congress or Executive Order either prohibits the practice, according to the Institute of Heraldry. The fringe on a Flag is considered an 'honorable enrichment only.' "

However, many out there in World Wide Web–ville see a sinister motivation behind this decorative addition. And so that I don't get accused of putting words in their mouths, here's a quote from a website with the rather apt URL of *gethatgoldfringeoffmyflag.com.*

It is commonplace to see a gold-fringed United States flag standing in the present-day courtrooms. Is the gold fringe there for decoration only, or does it signify a certain jurisdiction? Make no mistake about it—the American People have been put on notice that the normal constitutional functions of government have been suspended and that their Land has been placed under martial law. Just as you are aware that there are two "united states" one which is comprised of the "Republic states" and the other comprised of the "United States" which without authority of law incorporated itself in 1871 and 1874, are you aware that there are also two separate and distinct "flags" for each of these "united states" and it is the flag appearing within the sanctuary of the "bar" in court which determines the laws applying to that court?

FLAG #1: Flags with gold fringe, gold braid, gold eagle, gold spear, or gold ball atop the flagpole establishes the jurisdiction of the admiralty, maritime or administration jurisdiction. President Roosevelt describes this type of flag in 1933 and it's described by Army Regulation in 1979. This is an article 1 (one) jurisdiction court flag "guilty until proven innocent" war powers act. Indoors the gold-fringed flag only flies in military courts and therein when dealing with administrative matters are summary court martial proceedings against civilians.

FLAG #2: Article III (three) of the united states constitution describes the jurisdiction of the court by the American flag of peace under Title 4 U.S.C. 1. This flag is described as red, white and blue with stripes of red and white horizontally placed in alteration. Under the jurisdiction of the American flag of peace the united states constitution is alive and well and all rights are preserved. People are "innocent until proven guilty." The jurisdiction of the "American Flag" is the determining factor upon which all citizens rights are determined.

The solid gold-colored cords and tassels attached to the flagstaff, the finial, and the gold fringe on the flag itself, all taken together, indicate some undisclosed branch, division, or department of some undisclosed branch of the military services of the United States.

So is it "honorable enrichment"? Or a sinister plot? I leave the decision in your hands.

THE MEANING OF THE COLORS IN OUR FLAG

When I was in grammar school I remember having the colors of the flag explained to me: "The red is for the blood of the Minutemen; the white is for honesty; and the blue is for the ocean that we came across from England." Hardly an eloquent description, but I bought it hook, line, and sinker.

Something so revered as our flag is bound to generate myths and legends. For example, what *do* the colors of our flag mean? Surely they weren't chosen just because they look *nice* together?

One source quotes George Washington as saying: "We take the stars from heaven, and the red from our Mother Country, separating it by white stripes, thus showing that we have separated from her; and the white stripes shall go down to posterity representing liberty." Sounds grand, doesn't it?

The Stars of the Round Table

One of the many legends about our flag concerns the circular arrangement of the thirteen stars as seen on the "Betsy Ross" flag. Legend has it that the stars were arranged like this so that one state would not appear to have precedence over another—much like King Arthur's reasoning when he came up with the idea for his round table.

The "Round Table" flag with thirteen stars.

And don't think that you can determine which star stands for a particular state. It's easy to picture some teacher counting across the rows of stars and pointing to the nineteenth one, saying, "Students, this one represents Indiana, the nineteenth state to enter the Union." The fact is that the stars signify all fifty of our states in no particular order. The idea of designating each star to a specific state was proposed during discussions that led to the Flag Act of 1818, but the idea was rejected as "unwieldy."

But the Library of Congress, where Washington's papers are kept, has conducted a comprehensive search and were unable to find any mention of the great general "ever saying or writing it."

Here's another take on the colors, again attributed to

Charlie Duke

Charlie Duke was the module pilot for the Apollo 16 *crew—
he is one of the handful of men to have walked on the moon.*

Being a career U.S. Air Force officer, I have many memories of our
flag, Old Glory. I have always felt a great sense of pride every time
I saluted as it's been raised at military ceremonies.

None of these memories is more thrilling to me, however, than
when I had the rare honor of saluting our flag while standing on the
surface of the moon as a member of the *Apollo 16* crew. To see the
red, white, and blue silhouette against the blackness of the sky with
the earth hanging over it was truly a rare and extraordinary event.
Even after over thirty years I can still feel the pride course through
me. I still say the words I said then, "I'm proud to be an American!"

George Washington: "The white stripes represent the purity
and serenity of the nation, while the red stripes represent the
blood spilled by Americans who made the ultimate sacrifice
for freedom. The white stars symbolize the purity, liberty,
and freedom within the nation. The royal blue field stands
for freedom and justice. . . ." The quote goes on and on, but
I'm sure you get the drift.

There are as many interpretations of the colors of the flag
as there have been permutations in its appearance over its
history. One source claims the blue stands for heaven, the

white for the navy, and the red for the army. (Must be a football fan.) Another claims the red represents courage; the white, liberty; and the blue, loyalty. And yet another one claims that the red represents our wartime years, the white our peacetime years, and the blue stands for our faith in God.

The element of religion seems to recur quite often when looking into the stories of the history of our flag—and the present topic is no exception. A certain "manual of patriotism for boys and girls," published only a few years ago, claims that the colors "trace their ancestry back to Mount Sinai when the Lord gave Moses the Ten Commandments and the Book of the Law, and they were deposited in the Ark of the Covenant within the Tabernacle whose curtains were of scarlet, white, blue, and purple."

But the bottom line is, there is absolutely no historical basis for any meaning given to the colors of our flag. The best guess is that the red, white, and blue came from the colors devised for the Great Seal of the United States of America, the creation of which was authorized on July 4, 1776. In heraldic devices, such as seals, each element has a specific and detailed meaning. Charles Thompson, secretary of the Continental Congress, reporting to Congress on the Seal, stated: "The colors of the pales (the vertical stripes) are those used in the flag of the United States of America; White signifies purity and innocence, Red, hardiness & valour, and

Blue, the color of the Chief (the broad band above the stripes) signifies vigilance, perseverance & justice."

I think it's safe to say that the stories of the meaning of the colors of our flag actually stem from the description of the Great Seal. But we're still left with the question, "What do the colors of our flag stand for?" One doesn't need to devise specific meanings for each of the colors—one only needs to know that the Red, the White, and the Blue stand for one thing and one thing only—the United States of America.

CHAPTER EIGHT

The Flags of 9/11

*T*he first night of baseball's World Series championship game is always one of the most watched events in our country. On the night of October 27, 2001, however, as millions of fans watched from around the world, one battered and torn American flag, grimy with smoke and dust, stirred more emotions than any home run or triple play.

This flag had literally arisen like the phoenix from the ashes of the World Trade Center and has come to symbolize the spirit of Americans everywhere. When it was found in the rubble of the disaster site six weeks after the attack, twelve stars were missing from the field of blue. Most experts believe that this flag had been kept in one of the offices on the upper floors of the tower; it had somehow miraculously survived the firestorm of hot jet fuel that incinerated several stories of the building almost immediately.

That cool October night, as the New York Yankees, the Arizona Diamondbacks, and thousands of fans, including

Mayor Rudolph Giuliani and President George W. Bush stood on the field and in the stands, a moment of silence was observed in memory of those who died in the attacks on New York and the Pentagon and in the jet crash near Pittsburgh, Pennsylvania.

LEADING THE FLEET

A photo of the triumphant flag raising on the ruins of the World Trade Center seems destined to achieve the same type of immortality as did the World War II photo of the flag raising on the embattled Pacific island of Iwo Jima.

The photograph was taken on October 1, 2001. Three NYC firefighters, Dan McWilliams, George Johnson, and Billy Eisengrein had been digging in the rubble for more than six hours looking for survivors, to no avail. They were growing increasingly disheartened as they realized their rescue efforts had now become recovery efforts. In a burst of inspiration, the three men ran over to the Hudson River just a block away. There they found a 130-foot yacht aptly named *Star of America* owned by Shirley Dreifus, flying the flag while moored at one of the piers. They grabbed the flag off the boat and raced back to the site, where they raised it on a pole anchored in the rubble.

"Everyone just needed a shot in the arm," said McWilliams. "Every pair of eyes that saw that flag got a little brighter." Other firefighters concurred, saying that seeing

Where Has the World Trade Center Flag Gone?

The American flag that was raised by three firefighters over the wreckage of the World Trade Center, one of the most enduring images of September 11, has disappeared.

The flag, which had been taken from a yacht docked in the Hudson River by the firefighters who were later photographed raising it over the rubble, had been sent off to be flown on a number of naval ships serving in the war in Afghanistan. The flag was returned to New York officials in a solemn ceremony in March.

Just one problem: The flag that city officials have in their possession measures five feet by eight feet. The flag the firefighters raised on September 11 measured four feet by six feet, according to its original owners.

"It's just a really awkward and difficult situation," said a spokeswoman for the New York City mayor's office. "What it represents is really what's important."

The *New York Times* reported that city officials had traced the five-by-eight-foot flag as far back as a September 23 appearance in Yankee Stadium. They believe the original flag may have been accidentally switched or misplaced sometime between September 11 and that event.

★

their country's flag flying triumphantly atop the ruins was a much-needed inspiration.

The moment was captured on film by photographer Thomas E. Franklin of the Hackensack, New Jersey, paper *The Record*. The paper printed it the next day, and it was

The original flag came from a yacht, the *Star of America,* that was in a Hudson River marina near the World Trade Center that day. Firefighters working in the area took the flag and walked back to Ground Zero, where they raised it on a pole.

The discrepancy about the flag size was discovered when the yacht owners were preparing to formally donate the flag to the city.

"It's a mystery," said an attorney representing the owners. "Who knows what happened to it after the firefighters put it up and the photograph was taken. There was so much activity down there."

soon picked up by hundreds of other papers, news services, and network television.

"I knew by September 13 this was going to be a really popular picture," said Franklin, who has received thousands of e-mails from people detailing how the photo has touched them. "They said it made their day and lifted their spirits at a time of real despair."

About thirty thousand people have asked the newspaper for a copy, and thousands more are using it—without permission—for all sorts of purposes.

The photo has been downloaded, photocopied, airbrushed, screen-printed, sketched, and painted in homes and businesses across the country.

"It was a moment in an absolutely tragic, horrible day that seemed to rise above everything to symbolize the cooperation and spirit of New York, the country and the people at Ground Zero," said Frank Scandale, editor of *The Record*. "It gave people a sliver of hope in the most horrible, disastrous day any one of this generation can remember."

The flag itself was presented to Admiral Robert J. Natter, commander of the Atlantic fleet, by New York Governor George Pataki and Mayor Rudolph Giuliani. The two had signed the flag with an inscription reading in part: FDNY Division 1 World Trade Center.

Upon receiving the flag, Natter said, "This flag represents the spirit and courage of all Americans. It has incredible meaning for all our sailors and marines, and we're proud to fly it. . . . It will serve as both a remembrance and as a motivator for our . . . naval forces."

After the presentation, Admiral Natter flew with the flag to the aircraft carrier *Theodore Roosevelt* as it traveled to the Mideast war zone as part of Operation Enduring Freedom. The flag was flown from the mast atop the carrier and was then flown from the mast of each ship in the battle group.

Once its work in the Mideast was done, the *Theodore Roosevelt* returned to its homeport of Norfolk, Virginia. There, the flag was returned to two of the three firefighters in a solemn ceremony aboard the carrier. (The third, Dan McWilliams, was unable to be there because he was attending the funeral of a fellow firefighter killed in the 9/11 attack.)

On April 1, 2002, the flag was raised over City Hall in New

Army poster from World War I.

York City in another solemn ceremony marked by bagpipes playing "America the Beautiful."

"This flag has history, and I think it's very appropriate that it's here," said Police Commissioner Ray Kelly. "It means a lot to the city certainly at this time." The flag was flown over City Hall for a week, and then was circulated among police stations and firehouses throughout New York City. The fragile cloth was protected during its travels by a special case crafted for it by the navy.

INTO SPACE . . . BY ROCKET'S RED GLARE

An American flag pulled from the rubble of the World Trade Center as well as a U.S. Marine Corps flag that survived the attack on the Pentagon were flown into space aboard the space shuttle *Endeavour* as part of NASA's "Flags for Heroes and Families" campaign. The shuttle also carried thousands

Roma Downey

Roma Downey starred in Touched by an Angel.

I had the pleasure of attending the opening ceremony of the Winter Olympics 2002 in Salt Lake City.

As the Mormon Tabernacle Choir sang the national anthem, the tattered flag from the World Trade Center was carried out into the arena. Too fragile to be flown, it was gently held in a spotlight for all to see.

Then, as the choir sang on, the spotlight was dimmed and another one lit up on a pristine new flag being raised up a pole. By the time we heard the lyrics, "gave proof through the night that our flag was still there," we could see our flag shining, whole, born anew . . . like a phoenix arisen from the ashes.

The symbolism was not lost on the people who openly wept and then applauded. Everyone felt uplifted, strengthened, and inspired, for yes indeed, our flag *was* still there.

It was truly a memorable moment.

---

of smaller American flags that were later distributed to the victims' families and survivors of the September attacks.

"NASA wanted to come up with an appropriate tribute to the people who lost their lives in the tragic events of September 11," said NASA Administrator Daniel Goldin. "America's space program has a long history of carrying items into space to commemorate historic events, acts of courage and dramatic achievements. 'Flags for Heroes and Families' is a natural extension of this ongoing outreach project."

The legacy of flying American flags to space started in 1961 with the flight of the first American astronaut, Alan Shepard. Students from Cocoa Beach Elementary School in Florida purchased a flag from a local department store, which was later rolled up and placed between cables behind Shepard's head inside his *Freedom 7 Mercury* spacecraft.

A GERMAN NAVY SALUTE
TO THE AMERICAN FLAG

This is an e-mail from a young ensign aboard the guided missile destroyer ship *USS Winston Churchill* to his parents. Although the U.S. Navy has confirmed this story as factual, the author of the e-mail remains unknown.

Dear Dad,

We are still at sea. The remainder of our port visits have all been cancelled. We have spent every day since the attacks going back and forth within imaginary boxes drawn in the ocean, standing high-security watches, and trying to make the best of it. We have seen the articles and the photographs, and they are sickening. Being isolated, I don't think we appreciate the full scope of what is happening back home, but we are definitely feeling the effects.

About two hours ago, we were hailed by a German navy destroyer, *Lutjens* requesting permission to pass close by our port side. Strange, since we're in the middle of an empty ocean, but the captain acquiesced and we prepared to render them honors from our bridgewing. As they were making their approach, our conning officer used binoculars and announced that *Lutjens* was flying not the German, but the American flag. As she came alongside us, we saw the American flag flying half-mast and her entire crew topside standing at silent, rigid attention in their dress uniforms. They had made a sign that was displayed on her side that read "We Stand By You."

There was not a dry eye on the bridge as they stayed alongside us for a few minutes and saluted. It was the most powerful thing I have seen in my life. The German navy did an incredible thing for this crew, and it has truly been the highest point in the days since the attacks. It's amazing to think that only half-century ago things were quite different.

After *Lutjens* pulled away, the Officer of the Deck, who had been planning to get out later this year, turned to me and said, "I'm staying Navy." I'll write you when I know more about when I'll be home, but this is it for now.

Love you guys.

THE FLAGS ON MY BLOCK

Within a few days after the terrible events of September 11, 2001, I went out to buy a new American flag to hang over our front door. It soon became obvious that many others in our small town of Rye, New York, had the same idea—the first seven stores I went to had sold out their stock of flags within twenty-four hours of the tragedy. The frenzy was not limited to cloth flags, either; any merchandise that featured

★

Samuel Jay Rosenfeld
Samuel Jay Rosenfeld lives in London.

Old Glory for me symbolizes freedom, justice, and democracy, and as such belongs in all our hearts—as an Englishman I have often wondered why the American Revolution never crossed the Atlantic as this would have been a natural progression—but after September 11 you would never have guessed that—Old Glory is popping up everywhere. I would suspect that George Washington is having a good chuckle right now. On a lasting note, I think the United States and the United Kingdom stand together as a unifying family separated only by a common language. Long may the Stars and Stripes be a beacon to the world and let freedom sing from her shores on this sad day. Lset the world know we are one in all we do and that includes defending the right to be free.

God bless America.

★

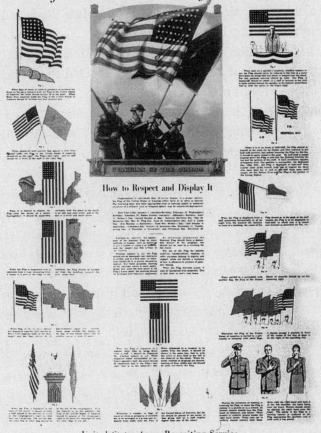

A poster on how to display the flag, created by the Office for Emergency Management during World War II.

the Stars and Stripes was vanishing from the shelves. The owner of our local hardware store told me that he had spent several hours rummaging through his storeroom to find any remaining Fourth of July stock and the few items he found were snapped up almost immediately.

I finally came upon one shop, which had just received a new shipment of cloth flags, and I selected the largest one that could fly from the pole over our front door. (In fact, this same flag still flies day and night at the front of our house, nearly a year and a half later—and, yes, I've made sure that it's properly illuminated during the hours from dusk until dawn.)

Once I finished hanging our flag that crisp September day, I stood back to admire my handiwork. How many of our neighbors showed the same patriotic spirit? I wondered to myself. I turned and looked down our street, only to see that I was late to the party. Almost every house on our block was already flying the flag—upon closer inspection I saw that the two houses that didn't feature a cloth flag had each displayed a paper flag in one of their windows.

One of the largest banners flew from the stoop of our next-door neighbors, Tom and Theresa Cahill, who came to this country from Ireland not long ago. Tom grew up on a farm in County Langford. He remembers visiting the village with his father one day when he was nine years old. As they walked down the cobbled streets he came upon a huge poster for the Cunard shipping line. The massive ocean liner in the poster seemed dwarfed by the enormous American flag flying from the tallest mast. This image struck a deep chord in the young boy. "Someday . . ." he thought to himself. That day finally came years later when he immigrated to America and found a job in construction. Several years after that Tom met and soon married another recent arrival from Ireland: Theresa, who had come from a farm in County Cavan. She still remembers the day when, as a young girl, she saw the American flag flying high over the U.S. embassy in Dublin— she, too, thought, "Someday . . ." In the best tradition of pursuing the American dream, this young couple worked hard to establish a home of their own in Rye, where they raised three daughters and two sons.

As I walked through our neighborhood, I marveled at the variety of flags that graced the fronts of houses—some on rods jutting out over front doors, others flying high from flagpoles set into cement in the little front yards, one even hanging from the branches of an elm tree. I realized that many of these houses belonged to families who had recently arrived in the United States as a result of job transfers: a Wall Street financial analyst and his young family from India had just purchased a house two streets over; an older couple from Japan owned the large Colonial across the street; and the Tudor a few blocks away had just become home to one of the world's foremost experts on multiple sclerosis—he and his wife were both from England.

As I stood there on my front porch, I thought back to the story of my own family.

My maternal grandmother, Anna Krupske, was a sixteen-year-old farm girl when she left her family in Alt Kristburg, Germany, and immigrated to the United States in the dank and crowded steerage section of the *SS Amerika*. As the massive ship pulled into New York harbor beneath the outstretched torch of the Statue of Liberty, a suave and solicitous gentleman offered to help her make her way to Pennsylvania Station so that she could catch her train to Colorado, where her older brother awaited her. Even though she could have used some help in getting from the dock to the train station, something in the fellow's manner seemed suspicious—he was just a bit *too* solicitous. After she had declined his help and he had wandered away to find someone else to assist, some of the older women on deck told her that her instincts had been correct—the suave fellow was a well-known solicitor for a white slavery ring operating out of New York.

Once she made it out to Colorado, she found things no easier there. She became a traveling seamstress, making her way from ranch to ranch. One morning she awoke to find that the rancher's wife for whom she was sewing had died during the night. The husband was off on a cattle drive hundreds of miles away. She scrawled a hasty note of explanation to him, then set off to find the nearest town by walking along the railroad tracks. Trudging all day on the plains under a merciless sun, the only water she could find was the rainwater in small puddles between the railroad ties. When I was a young boy she would tell my brothers and me this story, adding that the water was swarming with "leetle wriggling tings dat swam."

A few years later Anna made her way to Chicago, where she met and soon married another German immigrant, Auguste. This was during the early hysteria of World War I and so one night some drunken hooligans showed up at the young couple's door with a noose; they planned to hang my grandfather simply because he had a German surname. This memory brought to my mind the grim realization that things had not changed that much in America—in the few days since September 11 there had already been several reports of attacks on Americans of Middle Eastern heritage.

My father's side of the family shared a similar path to the promise of America. One of my ancestors, Baron Stransky, served in the court of the czar of Russia. One wintry day Baron Stransky requested a personal audience with the czar and once the two were alone, the young baron laid his cards on the table. It was apparent, he explained to the older leader, that the Russian people were beginning to chafe at the increasing hardships imposed upon them by the czar, especially the taxes that were growing by leaps and bounds. It wouldn't be long before scheming opportunists would jump in and start to incite rebellion and revolution, he warned. The czar would be ensuring his continued rule if he

This Is a Precious Thing

by Deborah Smoot, Salt Lake City, Utah

Grandma Butter was our next-door neighbor. The immigrant widow of a Polish baker, she had come to California because of the warm climate, because her ailing brother lived there, and probably, to be frank, because there was nowhere else for her to go. She lived in a Quonset hut next door to our Quonset hut, near the hospital where my doctor husband was doing his residency. But these were temporary lodgings for us, and I didn't see any need to become Grandma Butter's great friend.

We were so different. She was old, odd, and almost impossible to understand through her thick foreign accent. I was a working mother, full of myself, with little patience for an eccentric old woman.

It was our three-year-old son, Owen, who first befriended her. He couldn't begin to pronounce her long Polish surname, so he simply christened her "Grandma Butter." She rewarded his attention with her time and hard-sugar candies, and after a while he understood her words in spite of their chopped, guttural tones.

Every day she went about the same routine. Early each morning she began to prepare her brother's supper, cooking potatoes and cabbage on low heat in a covered pan on top of the stove, the smell wafting to us through her opened windows. She straightened up their small home, stacking up magazines, putting away her slippers, and watering a couple of straggly houseplants. Then she went outside to hang an American flag from three nails driven into the wooden post that held up their front porch.

Each afternoon our little boy waited by the screen door for a daily ceremony. At five o'clock Grandma Butter would come out on her front porch and signal for Owen to join her. Gently lifting him up, she let him unhook the flag from its nails. Then she would hand him two corners of the flag and he would help her fold it, like a little preschool Cub Scout. Holding this folded cotton flag in her arms for a moment, she would say to her little friend, "This is a precious thing."

My son is now fifteen years old and it's been many years since we lived in a Quonset hut. I don't even know where Grandma Butter is or if she's still alive. The last Christmas card we sent her came back with no forwarding address. In fact, I hadn't thought of Grandma Butter for a long time until I recently came across an old cotton flag at a garage sale. I bought it, and as I took it in my hands, I realized what she had held so close to her all those years ago—not just a faded, folded American flag, but what it symbolized.

I thought of my own great-grandmother, who, like Grandma Butter, emigrated to America. Young, widowed, and alone, sheltering two small children in the warmth of her coat, she must have been filled with fear. But she also took courage from the enormous possibilities before her.

Am I so different? I now have three children whom I sometimes wrap in my own coat on cool fall mornings at the high school soccer field. And for all my self-reliance, in the dark of night when I pray for my children, I am most of all a mother, scared, wanting to clutch them close to me like Grandma Butter with her flag in her arms. I am just like all of those before me who have somehow held and nurtured the precious notion of hope.

"This flag is for you, Grandma Butter," I wanted to say. "When I get home, we'll get out the hammer and the nails and hook it up on the beam by the garage. We'll put it up every morning and take it down each night. At the risk of appearing unsophisticated, we will conduct your unofficial flag ceremony. And, Grandma Butter, I will do my best to remember to tell the children, 'This is a precious thing.' "

were to relax the restrictions on the populace and allow them to keep a greater share of the crops and goods they produced. Unfortunately, the czar was less than receptive to Baron Stransky's prescient advice and ordered his guards to take him prisoner. In most cases like this, the offender would have been executed in short order, but young Stransky was very popular among the czar's court. Instead, the baron was exiled and was not allowed to take any of his considerable holdings with him.

The same skills that had served him so well in Russia helped him to reestablish himself in Bohemia, where he and his family became leading educators. I often wonder if he took any particular pleasure at the turn of events years after his exile, when Vladimir Ilyich Ulyanov—better known by his pseudonym, Lenin—incited the aggrieved Russian people to overthrow the czar.

One of Stransky's descendants shared his insight in realizing that the new world of America offered even more opportunities to make one's mark. He made his way to Racine, Wisconsin, where he became a successful community leader and started his family, which included my father.

My wife, Betty, can trace her family's arrival in America to the early eighteenth century, many years before the American flag even existed. In 1722, the three Renfrew brothers from Scotland arrived at a port in North Carolina. There the immigration officials misheard the name "Renfrew" as "Renfro." While two of the brothers settled in North Carolina, the third and youngest decided to travel west, following the Cumberland Trail into Kentucky. A few decades later some of the Kentucky Renfros moved up into southern Illinois, following the same path traveled by the family of Abraham Lincoln.

As I stood there on my front porch that September afternoon, I recognized the huge breadth of heritages that make up my family, the families on our street, and the families throughout our nation. Though each and every person who lives here can trace his or her ancestry to someplace else, we all now stand beneath one and the same flag—the flag that represents our United States of America and the words for which it stands: *E Pluribus Unum*—One Made Out of Many.

Following the Flag

*I*n early battles, soldiers literally followed their flag—it was the one signal element among the chaos of the battlefield that they could see at almost all times, and it indicated whether to advance or retreat. The role of flag-bearer was a highly honored one—after all, that person was the one to carry the very symbol of his nation or ruler into battle. Should the flag-bearer be struck down, many others were ready to pick up the colors again and carry on. Were the flag to completely vanish from sight, the spirits of the army would plummet in the knowledge that defeat was imminent.

Countless times over the past two hundred and twenty-seven years our fighting men and women have found it within themselves to rally yet again as they see the Stars and Stripes streaming before them. And every one of us—man or woman—stands ready to pick up those colors and carry on in defiance of any force or person who might mean us harm.

Since September 11, 2001, we Americans follow our flag

with a renewed sense of purpose and dedication. Though in substance a simple piece of cloth, it is freighted with the hopes, dreams, and blood of every one of us who honor and respect it. Just as the Bible can be considered as simply a collection of writings, it is seen as God's holy word by those who believe.

And so we follow the flag, as we have from the very beginning . . . trying our best, falling on our faces from time to time, but always making sure to keep in sight that shining goal so beautifully articulated by our Founding Fathers:

> We hold these truths to be self-evident, that all men are created equal, that they are endowed by their Creator with certain unalienable Rights, that among these are Life, Liberty, and the pursuit of Happiness . . .

I pray that we never lose sight of that goal—that courage and love of freedom woven throughout the tapestry that *is* our country—Old Glory.

The Federal Flag Code

The Federal Flag Code prescribes the proper display of and respect for the United States flag. Each state has its own flag law. Here is the code in its entirety (PUBLIC LAW 94–344):

JOINT RESOLUTION

To amend the joint resolution entitled "Joint resolution to codify and emphasize existing rules and customs pertaining to the display and use of the flag of the United States of America."

Resolved by the Senate and House of Representatives of the United States of America in Congress assembled, That the joint resolution entitled "Joint resolution to codify and emphasize existing rules and customs pertaining to the display and use of the flag of the United States of America," as amended (36 U.S.C. 171–178), is amended—

SEC. I That the following codification of existing rules and customs pertaining to the display and use of the flag of the United States of America be, and is hereby, established for the use of such civilians or civilian groups or organizations as may not be required to conform with regulations promulgated by one or more executive departments of the Government of the United States. The flag of the United States for the purpose of this chapter shall be defined according to title 4, United States Code, Chapter I, section I and section 2 and Executive Order 10834 issued pursuant thereto.

SEC. 2

(a) It is the universal custom to display the flag only from sunrise to sunset on buildings and on stationary flagstaffs in the open. However, when a patriotic effect is desired, the flag may be displayed twenty-four hours a day if properly illuminated during the hours of darkness.

(b) The flag should be hoisted briskly and lowered ceremoniously.

(c) The flag should not be displayed on days when the weather is inclement, except when an all weather flag is displayed.

(d) The flag should be displayed on all days, especially on New Year's Day, January 1; Inauguration Day, January 20; Lincoln's Birthday, February 12; Washington's Birthday, third Monday in February; Easter Sunday (variable); Mother's Day, second Sunday in May; Armed Forces Day, third Saturday in May; Memorial Day (half-staff until noon), the last Monday in May; Flag Day, June 14; Independence Day, July 4; Labor Day, first Monday in September; Constitution Day, September 17; Columbus Day, second Monday in October; Navy Day,

October 27; Veterans Day, November 11; Thanksgiving Day, fourth Thursday in November; Christmas Day, December 25; and such other days as may be proclaimed by the President of the United States; The birthdays of States (date of admission); and on State holidays.

(e) The flag should be displayed daily on or near the main administration building of every public institution.

(f) The flag should be displayed in or near every polling place on election days.

(g) The flag should be displayed during school days in or near every schoolhouse.

SEC. 3 That the flag, when carried in a procession with another flag or flags, should be either on the marching right; that is, the flag's own right, or, if there is a line of other flags, in front of the center of that line.

(a) The flag should not be displayed on a float in a parade except from a staff, or as provided in subsection (j).

(b) The flag should not be draped over the hood, top, sides, or back of a vehicle or of a railroad train or a boat. When the flag is displayed on a motor car, the staff should be fixed firmly to the chassis or clamped to the right fender.

(c) No other flag or pennant should be placed above or, if on the same level, to the right of the flag of the United States of America, except during church services conducted by naval chaplains at sea, when the church pennant may be flown above the flag during church services for the personnel of the Navy. (See Public Law 107, page 4)

(d) The flag of the United States of America, when it is displayed with another flag against a wall from crossed staffs, should be on the right, the flag's own right, and its staff should be in front of the staff of the other flag.

(e) The flag of the United States of America should be at the center and at the highest point of the group when a number of flags of States or localities or pennants of societies are grouped and displayed from staffs.

(f) When flags of states, cities, or localities, or pennants of societies are flown on the same halyard with the flag of the United States, the latter should always be at the peak. When the flags are flown from adjacent staffs, the flag of the United States should be hoisted first and lowered last. No such flag or pennant may be placed above the flag of the United States or to the United States flag's right.

(g) When flags of two or more nations are displayed, they are to be flown from separate staffs of the same height. The flags should be of approximately equal size. International usage forbids the display of the flag of one nation above that of another nation in time of peace.

(h) When the flag of the United States is displayed from a staff projecting horizontally or at an angle from the window sill, balcony, or front of a building, the union of the flag should be placed at the peak of the staff unless the flag is at half staff. When the flag is suspended over a sidewalk from a rope extending from a house to a pole at the edge of the sidewalk, the flag should be hoisted out, union first, from the building.

(i) When displayed either horizontally or vertically against a wall, the union should be uppermost and to the flag's own right, that is, to the observer's left. When displayed in a window, the flag should be displayed in the same way, with the union or blue field to the left of the observer in the street.

(j) When the flag is displayed over the middle of the street, it should be suspended vertically with the union to the north in an east and west street or to the east in a north and south street.

(k) When used on a speaker's platform, the flag, if displayed flat, should be displayed above and behind the speaker. When displayed from a staff in a church or public auditorium, the flag of the United States of America should hold the position of superior prominence, in advance of the audience, and in the position of honor at the clergyman's or speaker's right as he faces the audience. Any other flag so displayed should be placed on the left of the clergyman or speaker or to the right of the audience.

(l) The flag should form a distinctive feature of the ceremony of unveiling a statue or monument, but it should never be used as the covering for the statue or monument.

(m) The flag, when flown at half-staff, should be first hoisted to the peak for an instant and then lowered to the half-staff position. The flag should be again raised to the peak before it is lowered for the day. On Memorial Day the flag should be displayed at half-staff until noon only, then raised to the top of the staff. By order of the President, the flag shall be flown at half-staff upon the death of principal figures of the United States Government and the Governor of a State, territory, or possession, as a mark of respect to their memory. In the event of the death of other officials or foreign dignitaries, the flag is to be displayed at half-staff according to Presidential instructions or orders, or in accordance with recognized customs or practices not inconsistent with law. In the event of the death of a present or former official of the government of any State, territory, or possession of the United States, the Governor of that State, territory, or possession may proclaim that the National flag shall be flown at half-staff. The flag shall be flown at half-staff thirty days from the death of the President or a former President; ten days from the day of death of the Vice President, the Chief Justice or a retired Chief Justice of the United States, or the Speaker of the House of Representatives; from the day of death until interment of an Associate Justice of the Supreme Court, a Secretary of an executive or military department, a former Vice President, or the Governor of a State, territory, or possession; and on the day of death and the following day for a Member of Congress. As used in this subsection—

(1) the term "half-staff" means the position of the flag when it is one-half the distance between the top and bottom of the staff;

(2) the term "executive or military department" means any agency listed under sections 101 and 102 of title 5, United States Code; and

(3) the term "Member of Congress" means a Senator, a Representative, a Delegate, or the Resident Commissioner from Puerto Rico.

(n) When the flag is used to cover a casket, it should be so placed that the union is at the head and over the left shoulder. The flag should not be lowered into the grave or allowed to touch the ground.

(o) When the flag is suspended across a corridor or lobby in a building with only one main entrance, it should be suspended vertically with the union of the flag to the observer's left upon entering. If the building has more than one main entrance, the flag should be suspended vertically near the center of the corridor or lobby with the union to the north, when entrances are to the east and west or to the east when entrances are to the north and south. If there are entrances in more than two directions, the union should be to the east.

SEC. 4 That no disrespect should be shown to the flag of the United States of America; the flag should not be dipped to any person or thing. Regimental colors, State flags, and organization or institutional flags are to be dipped as a mark of honor.

(a) The flag should never be displayed with the union down, except as a signal of dire distress in instances of extreme danger to life or property.

(b) The flag should never touch anything beneath it, such as the ground, the floor, water.

(c) The flag should never be carried flat or horizontally, but always aloft and free.

(d) The flag should never be used as wearing apparel, bedding, or drapery. It should never be festooned, drawn back, nor up, in folds, but always allowed to fall free. Bunting of blue, white, and red, always arranged with the blue above, the white in the middle, and the red below, should be used for covering a speaker's desk, draping the front of the platform, and for decoration in general.

(e) The flag should never be fastened, displayed, used, or stored in such a manner as to permit it to be easily torn, soiled, or damaged in any way.

(f) The flag should never be used as a covering for a ceiling.

(g) The flag should never have placed upon it, nor on any part of it, nor attached to it any mark, insignia, letter, word, figure, design, picture, or drawing of any nature.

(h) The flag should never be used as a receptacle for receiving, holding, carrying or delivering anything.

(i) The flag should never be used for advertising purposes in any manner whatsoever. It should not be embroidered on such articles as cushions or handkerchiefs and the like, printed or otherwise impressed on paper napkins or boxes or anything that is designed for temporary use and discard. Advertising signs should not be fastened to a staff or halyard from which the flag is flown.

(j) No part of the flag should ever be used as a costume or athletic uniform. However, a flag patch may be affixed to the uniform of military personnel, firemen, policemen, and members of patriotic organizations. The flag represents a living country and is itself considered a living thing. Therefore, the lapel flag pin being a replica, should be worn on the left lapel near the heart.

(k) The flag, when it is in such condition that it is no longer a fitting emblem for display, should be destroyed in a dignified way, preferably by burning.

SEC. 5 During the ceremony of hoisting or lowering the flag or when the flag is passing in a parade or in review, all persons present except those in uniform should face the flag and stand at attention with the right hand over the heart. Those present in uniform should render the military salute. When not in uniform, men should remove their headdress with their right hand and hold it at the left shoulder, the hand being over the heart. Aliens should stand at attention. The salute to the flag in a moving column should be rendered at the moment the flag passes.

SEC. 6 During rendition of the national anthem when the flag is displayed, all present except those in uniform should stand at attention facing the flag with the right hand over the heart. Men not in uniform should remove their headdress with their right hand and hold it at the left shoulder, the hand being over the heart. Persons in uniform should render the military salute at the first note of the anthem and retain this position until the last note. When the flag is not displayed, those present should face toward the music and act in the same manner they would if the flag were displayed there.

SEC. 7 The Pledge of Allegiance to the Flag, "I pledge allegiance to the Flag of the United States of America, and to the Republic for which it stands, one Nation under God, indivisible, with liberty and justice for all," should be rendered by standing at attention facing the flag with the right hand over the heart. When not in uniform men should remove their headdress with their right hand and hold it at the left shoulder, the hand being over the heart. Persons in uniform should remain silent, face the flag, and render the military salute.

SEC. 8 Any rule or custom pertaining to the display of the flag of the United States of America, set forth herein, may be altered, modified, or repealed, or additional rules with respect thereto may be prescribed, by the Commander-in-Chief of the Armed Forces of the United States, whenever he deems it to be appropriate or desirable; and any such alteration or additional rule shall be set forth in proclamation.

Acknowledgments

Without the help of the following people, this book would not have come into being. For their support I'm immensely grateful.

My wife, Betty, who didn't mind the American flag becoming a third party in our household.

My son Peter, whose incisive research, insight, and creative input made this book possible.

My son Kit, the history buff, whose knowledge was invaluable.

My father, Arthur, who instilled respect for the flag in me at an early age.

My father-in-law, Rolla Renfro, who enlivened history for me.

Jennifer Brehl, my editor and daughter-in-law, who went beyond the call of duty in overseeing this book's content and schedule.

My brothers, Herb and Don, who followed the flag in naval service.

Sharon Azar, my assistant, always there for help.

The librarians in Rye, New York, for their assistance.

And finally, to all those wonderful people whose memories and thoughts about our country's flag grace the pages of this book.

Illustration Credits

Thanks to the following parties for permission to include photographs and other illustrations in this book:

Betsy Ross House, Philadelphia: page 29.

Metropolitan Museum of Art: page 10.

NASA: color plate 10.

National Archives: pages 13, 16, 19, 24, 30, 34, 37, 44 (both), 46, 50, 51, 58 (both), 59, 97, 117, 119, 120, 144, 157, 166, and 171; color plates 1, 2, 3, 4, 5, 6, 7, 8, 11, and 12.

National Archives, photograph by P. Bonn: page 87.

National Archives (Brady Collection), photographs by Mathew Brady: pages 49, 53, and 137.

National Archives, photograph by John Full: page 69.

National Archives, photograph by Dorothea Lange: page 92.

National Archives, photograph by J. Rosenthal, AP (1945): page 122.

Richard H. Schneider: pages iv and 2.

Starad, Inc., photograph by Christopher Radko: color plate 9.